GUIDANCE MONOGRAPH SERIES

Shelley C. Stone

Bruce Shertzer

Editors

GUIDANCE MONOGRAPH SERIES

The general purpose of Houghton Mifflin's Guidance Monograph Series is to provide high quality coverage of topics which are of abiding importance in contemporary counseling and guidance practice. In a rapidly expanding field of endeavor, change and innovation are inevitably present. A trend accompanying such growth is greater and greater specialization. Specialization results in an increased demand for materials which reflect current modifications in guidance practice while simultaneously treating the field in greater depth and detail than commonly found in textbooks and brief journal articles.

The list of eminent contributors to this series assures the reader expert treatment of the areas covered. The monographs are designed for consumers with varying familiarity to the counseling and guidance field. The editors believe that the series will be useful to experienced practitioners as well as beginning students. While these groups may use the monographs with somewhat different goals in mind, both will benefit from the treatment given to content areas.

The content areas treated have been selected because of specific criteria. Among them are timeliness, practicality, and persistency of the issues involved. Above all, the editors have attempted to select topics which are of major substantive concern to counseling and guidance personnel.

Shelley C. Stone

Bruce Shertzer

APPALACHIAN STUDENTS AND GUIDANCE

JAMES C. HANSEN
STATE UNIVERSITY OF NEW YORK AT BUFFALO

RICHARD R. STEVIC
STATE UNIVERSITY OF NEW YORK AT BUFFALO

HOUGHTON MIFFLIN COMPANY · BOSTON
NEW YORK · ATLANTA · GENEVA, ILL. · DALLAS · PALO ALTO

Library of Congress Catalog Card
Number: 78-150389
ISBN: 0-395-12437-9

COPYRIGHT © 1971 BY HOUGHTON MIFFLIN COMPANY. *All rights reserved. No part of this work may be reproduced or transmitted in any form or by any means, electronic or mechanical, including photocopying and recording, or by any information storage or retrieval system, without permission in writing from the publisher. Printed in the U.S.A.*

CONTENTS

EDITORS' INTRODUCTION ... vii

AUTHORS' INTRODUCTION ... ix

1. *A Profile of the People* ... 1
2. *Education and Work* ... 20
3. *Organization of Guidance Services* ... 30
4. *Counselor Preparation for Appalachia* ... 44
5. *Guidance for Appalachia* ... 54

BIBLIOGRAPHY ... 71

INDEX ... 75

EDITORS' INTRODUCTION

Appalachia. To many the word conjures up vignettes of a breed of men — sturdy mountaineers, moonshiners, revenuers — who, though somewhat mysterious, were liked and admired for their independence and hardiness. But for many who live within Appalachia, this romantic picture is far from reality. Their reality is grimly frustrating and their outlook bleak. Poverty has denied them what others have taken for granted. The penalties of poverty are always severe. Compared with their contemporaries, the poor appear always to have shorter lives, more illness, more physical and emotional defects, more personal crises, less education, less opportunity for improvement, and less protection from hazards.

Poverty may be defined as the inability or failure of an individual or a family to obtain the necessary income to sustain the minimum customary level of living at a given time or place. In 1964, President Lyndon B. Johnson declared "unconditional war on poverty in America." This ringing declaration was soon followed by the adoption of the Appalachian Regional Development Act by Congress in 1965. Special assistance for the eleven states included in this area was provided by the act. This assistance took many forms — road building, water and flood control, the construction of vocational training and health facilities, programs to improve livestock, and lumbering and coal mining operations — and the hope was that the Appalachian pocket of poverty would be eliminated.

While this monograph points out that not all of Appalachia is poor, the predominant group described within its profile of peoples is one that the wheel of fortune has bypassed. And it should be noted that what is only a "wheel of fortune" for an individual or a family is a spinning wheel of irreversible underdevelopment for a geographic region.

The authors — James C. Hansen and Richard R. Stevic — have sought to infer from their profile of Appalachian people the kind of guidance program and the kind of school counselors that would serve best the interests of such a clientele. Further, they offer some observations about preparing counselors to be able to extend helping relationships to students, parents, and teachers in this geographic region. Because this region covers eleven states, the material presented by the authors has application for a large segment of the population.

SHELLEY C. STONE

BRUCE SHERTZER

AUTHORS' INTRODUCTION

In 1959, when Congress authorized expenditure of large sums of money for the expansion of guidance services, impetus was given to the development of guidance and personnel in the schools. Although primarily concerned with identification of students with high academic potential, the National Defense Education Act was also directed toward providing assistance for all students in achieving their potential.

As a result of the emphasis and growth of guidance services, several groups of people have been identified as needing specialized assistance. These groups include the inner city poor, rural poor, black Americans, American Indians, Spanish-speaking Americans, and, the focus of this monograph, Appalachian whites. A major difficulty is that these groups do not have the power to develop ways of improving their own lives nor can they influence those who could provide help. The publicizing of their situation during the past decade may have intensified the problems by promoting the expectations of a comprehensive solution.

The providing of guidance services for the Appalachian population is one facet of a total approach for the improvement of educational, vocational, and personal opportunities. Training for those who are to be engaged in this effort, whether as school teachers, counselors, or administrators, must deal with the uniqueness of Appalachia. Educators must begin to develop didactics and procedures to aid school personnel in relating to the youth of this region. Traditionally, the schools of Appalachia have not received the necessary monetary or personal support from county, state, and national organizations. This situation must be reversed.

We have attempted to provide a generalized approach to the provision of meaningful guidance and counseling assistance in Appalachia. The first two chapters present an overview of the Appalachian culture. The remaining chapters focus on how guidance services can help improve the lives of Appalachian youth. We do not expect that any program would reflect the suggestions of this monograph in its entirety. However, we do believe that the issues which are raised and discussed have relevance to most counselors working with Appalachian students.

JAMES C. HANSEN

RICHARD R. STEVIC

The Appalachian Region

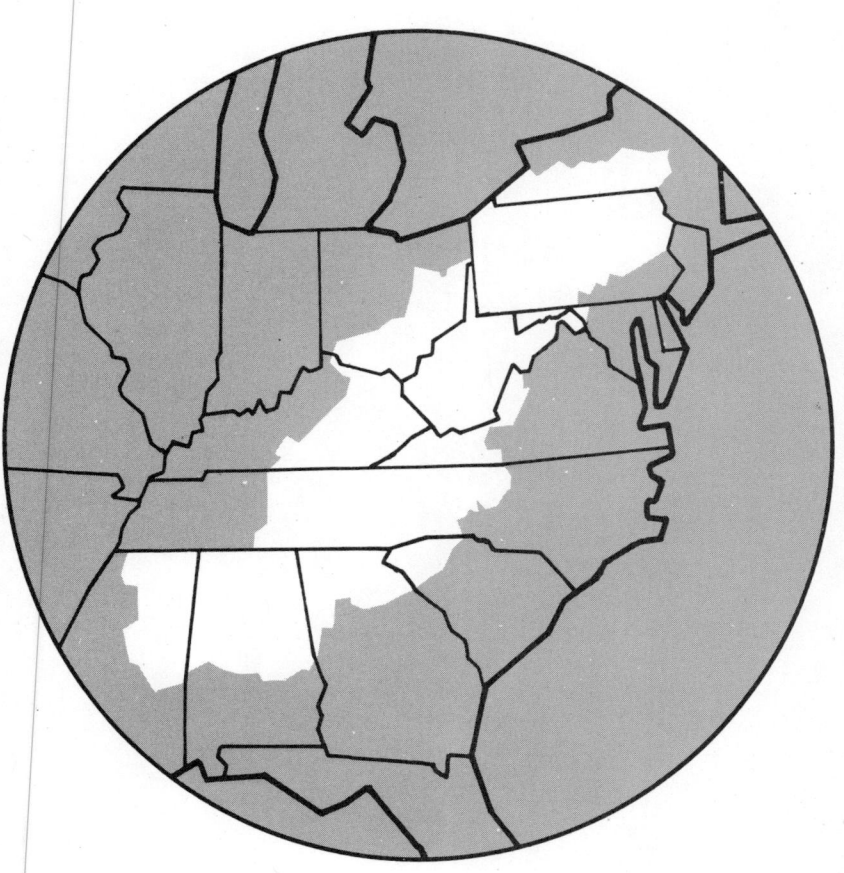

1

A Profile of the People

Appalachia

The Appalachian region includes portions of Alabama, Georgia, Kentucky, Maryland, Mississippi, New York, North Carolina, Ohio, Pennsylvania, South Carolina, Tennessee, and Virginia, and all of West Virginia. This is a vast region running from northeast to southwest along the Appalachian mountain chain, which extends for 1,300 miles from Vermont to northern Alabama. The chain is a series of relatively low but steep mountain ranges.

Appalachia has been described as a region of great beauty, majestic scenery, and startling landscapes. It is inhabited by people of great inner fortitude who are dignified, proud, and strongly loyal to tradition. It has been called a region of great opportunity because of its rich natural resources of coal, timber, gas, oil, stone, clay, and salt. It once abounded with wild life and its streams were a fisherman's dream.

Part of the problem in Appalachia is that the people have not reaped the rewards of the area's natural wealth. It has suffered for many years as a result of isolation, lack of transportation and access to more highly developed neighboring areas, sweeping shifts away from farming and mining, and inadequate public facilities and services.

Caudill (1965) states that long ago Appalachia was rich and green, but for years it has been sick and now it is dying, a charity patient of affluent America. It is a mammoth island of backwardness and most of its people are paupers. Its economy generates much wealth and much poverty. The wealth flows outward to different cities and the poverty accumulates at home. Many communities in Appalachia are poorly built and are without decent schools, hospitals, or roads. In the past decade the communities have turned into people sties. At least two-thirds of the existing housing is dilapidated. Most of the population is spread out in towns that are found in winding creek valleys. Many Appalachian dwellers are clustered in crumbling coal camps. These communities lack adequate water supplies, and the available water is frequently polluted. The demoralized people have littered the roadsides and streams with countless automobile bodies and trash dumps. The creeks and rivers are reeking sewers. "New generations are born into the old relentless cycle of poor people, poor schools, poor job preparation, poor pay and more poor people."

Interest in the area is created not because Appalachia is underdeveloped and is not making a great economic contribution, but rather because of the deprived living status of its people. Appalachian people are similar to other chronic low-income families that have a distinct culture. There are differences between people in poverty who have enjoyed some financial success and lost it, and those who have never had it. Although both groups exist in Appalachia, the predominant group is the one that has never really been out of the low-income category (John, 1965).

Over 18 million people live in Appalachia and 93% of them are white. There are counties where more than a third of the population is unemployed and where government checks, social security, welfare, and aid to dependent children are the prime source of income. Some men are so far from their last job that they cannot properly be described as having a trade. The average adult has a sixth grade education. Three-fourths of the children who start school drop out before they complete the twelfth grade (Schrag, 1968).

The remoteness of a sizeable number of people with the lower educational and skill levels which usually accompany such isolation, offers a major obstacle to Appalachian prosperity. One development which is indicative of the problem is that the distribution of urban-rural population in Appalachia is just the reverse of the total United States. Over three-fifths of all Americans outside Appalachia live in metropolitan areas; in Appalachia almost three-fifths of the people live in a rural or semi-rural environment. The large cities of the country are centers of economic activity and generate the high standard of living that is generally enjoyed. In the last century there has been a major increase in job opportunities located in metropolitan areas and a substantial decline in other areas. The same thing is true in the Appalachian area. The job growth that has occurred in Appalachia during the past two decades has been confined almost exclusively to the metropolitan areas and to smaller towns which are sufficiently strong to attract new employment opportunities (Sweeney, 1968).

Until about 1948, coal was a huge industry. As a mass employer it was beset by oil and gas and advancing mining technology. Scores of coal companies were forced out of business during the 1950's and those remaining in operation were forced to mechanize to an astounding degree. Therefore, most of the industrial workmen were left stranded in mining communities. These were men who had been educated for the mines; their communities were poorly built and without adequate schools, hospitals, or roads. Mine employment in the 1950's fell 60%, rail employment fell with the decline of coal mining, and farming as a source of jobs dropped 50%. There was a massive migration from Appalachia.

In the 1960's despair set in. Efforts to attract industry to Appalachia met with little success. The hardest-hit areas were only accessible by narrow, unserviced, twisting mountain roads. In the middle sixties the region had attracted some attention and a joint State-Federal Appalachian Regional Commission was established to develop a program intended to meet the needs of this entire region. In 1965 Congress approved an Appalachian Regional Development Act authorizing the expenditure of $840 million over a six-year period for highways plus an additional $252 million over a two-year period for other projects. The 1967 Congress raised the highway authorization to a little over one billion but provided only $70 million for non-highway projects in the second two-year period. There were additional funds from the "war on poverty" programs.

The people have long been dependent on public assistance for their livelihood. Many miners still earn a subsistence by digging coal from the thin seams with hand tools. These operations lack the protection of a Federal mine safety code and are in hopeless competition with strip mines and large mechanized operations.

The concept of the company store, although perhaps valuable at the time, has been a debilitating influence to several generations of out-of-work miners. The dependence which was fostered by the company store kept the miner from having to deal with normal living problems and prevented his learning constructive ways to order his own affairs. His indebtedness, in many cases, created a situation where everything he had or earned would be claimed by the owner of the store. Thus, while he might once have had the motivation and desire to work, he quickly found that it did not really pay. Subsequent generations have apparently not challenged the new way of life which welfare or government doles create.

One of the greatest needs of the Appalachian people is education. The schools are poor and often abominable, and most of the country's one-room schools are in the highland counties. The adult illiteracy is appallingly high. Teachers' salaries are well below the national averages, and many of the better teachers have moved away.

Not all of Appalachia is poor. There are growth centers within the region which are prosperous. Schools, hospitals, libraries, and other public facilities and services in these areas are good. However, such islands of affluence are located in a sea of poverty and they grow as much by attracting people from other parts of the country as by drawing people out of the surrounding countryside.

Progress

There are signs of progress. Employment is rising slowly but steadily, and the number of people on welfare has fallen. Not as many people are leaving the area, and efforts are being made to attract new industry. The younger generation is finding opportunity in vocational schools or colleges to be trained for a different way of life.

Although the Federal poverty program was aimed at all indigenous Americans, Appalachia is one of the symbols. As a consequence, special funds have been appropriated for construction of highways, water facilities, and hospitals. Distribution of food has been augmented through a food stamp program which enables the poor to purchase more groceries than their welfare checks would otherwise permit. Unemployed fathers have been given jobs in a work experience training program. Young men and women have enrolled in Job Corps and Neighborhood Youth Corps programs. Vocational education has received increased support, and large sums have been made available for education. The effects of these programs on Appalachia are clear: new roads and vocational schools are in use or under construction; medical facilities are more accessible; the school dropout rate has been reduced; there are fewer obvious signs of malnutrition. Federal support in terms of education through job training has provided people with opportunities to earn money while receiving training or education. However, for many others the existing programs serve only to hide the misery. The new highways make it possible to cross large portions of Appalachia without seeing the tarpaper shacks or the coal dumps. Food stamps run out before the end of the month, and the schools, although far better than they used to be, still remain a blind alley.

The economic revival in Appalachia is due to exogenous forces. Accelerated growth in our national economy and Federal regional development programs explains the reduction in unemployment and the rise in income in this region. But the unemployment rate in Appalachia is still substantially above the national average while per capita income remains below it. Assuming that the trends of the past few years will continue, the growth rate in the Appalachian economy will probably be slightly below that of the nation as a whole. This is not enough. The growth rate of Appalachia should be slightly higher than the national economy, if the region is to catch up with national averages. This will require more vigorous leadership than has been witnessed to date. Continued balance between rural and urban population, an improved educational system, reorganization of archaic county governments, overhaul of regressive and ineffective tax systems, and control of the environment are necessary if Appalachian development is to speed up (Miernyk, 1968).

People

Writers who concentrate on Appalachia frequently devote most of their attention to the mountain population, partly because it is a sizeable contingent, partly because its existence has been defined as "a social problem," and partly because the rest of the region's people are too much like most Americans to be considered "interesting" (Ford, 1962).

Weller (1968) suggests that there are widespread differences in culture in Appalachia. One of the difficulties in writing about any group in a geographical area is that it is by no means socially homogeneous. There is a middle class and a professional class in the mountains, and both have much of the same characteristics as these classes anywhere else. They contrast with the folk class which exists along side them. One cannot assume that all the people living within Appalachia bear the stamp of the folk culture. However, most of the people living within Appalachia have come out of this folk culture and so share in it as a background.

From Weller's (1965b) description of "yesterday's people" we see the Appalachian people as highly individualistic but not independent. They want for themselves but are not deeply concerned with people or events which are not directly related to their own well-being. They are also oriented toward tradition, holding on to those things with which they are familiar, and hesitant to accept solutions to their persisting problems. They are somewhat fatalistic, capitalizing upon their fatalism as a kind of buffer against failure and disappointment in life.

They are action-oriented, reject the routine, and avoid long-term commitments. They are fearful of being left out of things and anxious to be accepted in their family group.

We, too, are going to focus on the folk culture. Besides being somewhat unique, it is this group that has experienced the greatest physical, social, and economic frustrations. In addition, most people in the region share some of this culture and those who migrate take the folk ways with them. For these reasons we will examine some of the roles which the church, school, and family play in this culture. A better understanding of this background should assist a counselor in providing guidance services.

Some writers suggest that much of the area was settled by debtors and they have never gotten out of the habit. Caudill (1963) suggests that the principal settlers in eastern Kentucky were orphans, debtors, and criminals who were sent from the British Isles to the New World to work in the tobacco plantations. After working off their passage, many fled to the Appalachian highlands. They brought with them little formal education, few religious beliefs, a limited sense of social obligations, no government of any form, and a fierce belief in individualism. This background is considerably different from the New England settler who was strongly religious and who quickly created some form of government.

The Appalachian mountaineer looked to himself and his family for handling civil cases. As for criminal acts, the only crimes he recognized were those against himself or his family as he had no concern with crime against the larger society. He did not care what his neighbors did as long as he was not bothered. This individualism exists to an amazing degree today (John, 1965).

The isolation of the area permitted this individualism to survive. The mountains sheltered the development of a separate culture in a time when mass media communication and travel developed in other parts of the country. While the rest of the nation experienced a technological revolution, the Appalachian region continued to use technological and social antiques. Individualism and isolation have been strong influences in the development of this low-income culture.

The Appalachian highlander is generally not a joiner of organizations. This is primarily because he values his individualism and because he has not needed the group for his activities. The only group that seems to be of major importance is the family. The family ties are exceptionally strong, but families are not ordered into formal organizations. They do not have the problem of many urbanites who form a committee before they can act. Most decisions are made cooperatively between family and kin.

These historical and cultural factors have formed a value system that is supported to a remarkable degree by both the social and economic factors of the Appalachian society. The historical value of individualism, the geographical isolation, the predominance of extractive industry, the exposure to long periods of low income, and the lack of group experiences have all made their impact upon this culture.

The low income orientation of the culture is not a lack of motivation to do better, but actually represents an adjustment to reality. People are not motivated because goals do not seem obtainable, and this lack of opportunity supports the value system and tends to perpetuate it. Many people in Appalachia have little chance of ever obtaining high incomes regardless of their motivation.

Perhaps the most remarkable aspect of this value system is not that it exists, but the fact that nearly all aspects of Appalachian life and experiences support it. Most value systems contain certain amounts of built-in conflicts. However, in Appalachia the historical background of the people, the economic and social structures, the religion, the political system, and even the schools support the value system. The only evident conflict is with the rest of the American value system. The strong supportive bonds of the Appalachian value system permit it to resist effectively the probes of the outside system. Psychologically, the outside value system is rejected as being undesirable and the Appalachian culture is viewed as being good. It appears that the more the Appalachian culture and values are attacked publicly the more the people reconfirm their basic beliefs and resist the outside influences.

The strength of the value system has not been broken by education or migration. Many migrants leave the area only to form Appalachian communities within other cities. Others find life on the outside unbearable and soon return to the lesser opportunity but, psychologically, greater security at home. Those leaving the area for college or military service often return and slip easily into the old pattern of life. It is this kind of interaction that leads to the observation that you can take the boy out of the mountains, but you can't take the mountains out of the boy.

It is not unusual in many areas of Appalachia to see weekly caravans of cars heading North to jobs on Sunday evening and returning to the homestead on Friday evening. The strong affiliation which the Appalachian has to the area is both an admirable and a debilitating trait. In many instances the only real hope which the person has of breaking the hold which poverty has on him is to leave, and yet the Appalachian often cannot do this. Thus, the cycle of poverty and undeveloped human potential remains unbroken.

Most authors describing this region, and particularly the regional planners, admit to difficulty in understanding and dealing with the values they encounter. They wonder how the people can resign themselves to acceptance of minimal welfare payments as a way of life. They often ask why the people are not more eager to leave their hopeless environment for urban areas with greater opportunity. They look for an explanation for the lack of ambition, the "episodic" view of life, and the inability of the people to arouse themselves to productive efforts. Ball (1968) suggests that what the observer cannot easily understand is the daily experience of inexorable pressure, insoluble problems, and absolutely overwhelming frustration. These are experiences of the poor generally, but they have been experienced with intensity by the mountaineer. Ball states that the southern Appalachian folk subculture represents to a significant degree the institutionalization of frustration-instigation behavior. The principal values, beliefs, and norms of behavior formed during a history of protracted misfortune are supported by the internal nature of the subculture and the external pressures of contemporary life. The young learn to anticipate defeat and to develop the subcultural attitudes that reduce its impact. Ball contends that to explain, predict, and alter their behavior, one must recognize the extent to which it reflects the institutionalized, non-rational response to frustration which he terms "analgesic." This reaction is frustration-instigated rather than motivation-instigated. One would therefore predict that the Appalachian folk subculture would be dominated by symptoms of fixation, aggression, and resignation.

Fixation as a subcultural pattern may help explain much of the obstinate traditionalism of the southern Appalachian folk culture. What has been criticized as stubbornness and adherence to old ways becomes more understandable in terms of the soothing qualities of ritual. Those who complain that the tenacious adherence to custom limits the adaptability of the subculture are quite correct, but this behavior may be temporarily effective in reducing anxiety. The result is that although the opinionated, dogmatic, and argumentative behavior of the mountaineer may multiply his problems, he persists in it nevertheless. This irrationality is at least comprehensible as a frustration-instigated reaction.

The frustration-instigated behavior concept also helps to predict that this subculture is typified by patterns of regression, aggression, and resignation. Many of these behaviors describing the folk subculture can be construed as examples of regression induced by frustration. These characteristics would include the lack of aesthetic appreciation, anti-intellectualism, the preference of anecdote to abstraction, the insistence upon the literal interpretation of the Bible, the entanglement of religious fundamentalism with deep superstition, the imprudent squandering which often accompanies payday, the tendency for self-pity and the "sick role" which local physicians sometimes term a "chronic passive-dependency syndrome."

Two particular manifestations of regressive behavior stand out. One of these may be called the welfare syndrome and the other familialism. Many members of the folk subculture have regressed to a state of social dependency. What had been intended as temporary assistance has been converted into a way of life. The satisfaction which occurs from frustration-instigated behavior is in the form of relief rather than goal attainment, and the literature on Appalachian life consistently points to the intensive emotional dependence on family. Many young people do not establish themselves as separate individuals nor are they encouraged to do so by their parents. Grown offspring who dislike their parents cannot bear to move away from them. Migrants who have finally broken away return home suddenly at the slightest misfortune. The subculture not only condones this behavior but continues to institutionalize it.

Much of the conduct of the mountaineer is comprehensible in terms of the aggression in the pattern. This helps to explain the infamous mountain feuds. Feuding behavior is an excellent example of the subculture's patterned behavior, which, while providing the momentary satisfactions of revenge, serves no rational purpose. The feud was not developed as an intelligently designed means to an end nor even as an accidentally effective instrument. The expression of aggression is interpreted as a tension-reducing response against available objects rather than as a rationally motivated, goal-directed activity.

Resignation, apathy, and fatalism are part of the subculture pattern. Resignation consists of giving up. It is not representative of goal-oriented behavior. In fact, goals are divorced from reality, and motivation seems largely absent. Resignation has the attributes of the other frustration-instigated behaviors. It is not a means to anything but an end-of-the-line behavior. Such a response may be difficult for motivation-oriented observers to understand but it is quite likely to provide relief from the tensions of extreme and prolonged frustration.

The southern Appalachian folk culture is easier to understand in terms of the thesis that Ball presents. "Responding to a given configuration of 'insoluble problems,' the mountaineer has developed a way of life emphasizing stereotyped behavior, dependency, belligerence, and fatalistic resignation. Admittedly, these reactions are not adequate adaptations to the situation." They do not represent a constructive coping with the environment. Nevertheless, their responses are in a limited sense functional, for they provide relief from the pains of frustration. Persons who would modify these subcultural behaviors must realize that they may be for some the only emotional refuge available. They must also realize that to stigmatize such practices may simply reinforce them.

The impoverished mountaineer has been faced with increasing frustrations deriving from the sense of relative deprivation and the growing urgency that he solve his problems. The concept of relative deprivaton is forced upon him through increasing physical contact with other people and by way of mass media. These convey an image of the "good life" and, in contrast, his own existence appears more bleak and hopeless than before. His frustrations are also deepened by those who urge him to self-help and increase his expectations for improvement, for they may succeed in increasing his desire for a "better life." Unless this goal is attained quickly, the problem often becomes even more frustrating simply because the motivation to solve it is intensified.

Family

There is no such thing as the typical Appalachian family. Within this region there are many different family profiles. These include well educated people living in large cities, lower-class whites and blacks, middle-class whites and blacks, farm families, mining families, inner-city families, isolated hollow families and so on. There is no more a typical Appalachian family than any other typical American family. One must take care not to paint the region with the broad strokes of a single brush as if it were a homogeneous area.

The Appalachian family structure is a natural outgrowth of the history of the area. The particular structures of these families served well to enable them to cope with the situations which they faced during the centuries of Appalachian isolation. However, Appalachian families have not changed fast enough to cope with the changing economy and have found themselves with cultural forms that are not working as well today as they did yesterday.

The first characteristic of the mountain family is its strong sense of itself as a unit for training, socializing, and action. The first responsibility of an individual is toward his kin. The Appalachian family is no longer noticeably larger than average families anywhere, although they still do have some fairly large families. Among mountain families, in general, the birth rate would be fairly close to the national average. Traditionally, mountain families had to depend upon themselves for almost everything; thus the family became geared to its own life. They were doctors, implement makers, tailors, engineers, and teachers. Since travel was not easy, members of the family settled close to one another in the same valley, and as children married they built their homes near those whom they depended upon for everything in their life. This close interrelation was a strength for them. Children were brought up in the midst of grandparents, aunts, uncles, cousins. The children were expected to help in the family tasks of farming or homemaking and at one time even in the mine. This bound them together very closely and developed a phenomenon called familialism. Each member of the family assumed he belonged first and foremost to his family and the children were brought up with this concept. Of course during the period of booming coal production it was desirable for the mine owner and miner to have family groups producing an unending stream of laborers.

Most of the community activities in the isolated areas are still carried out in this family structure. Persons from the outside coming into the region may see a society without any structure, yet various families give a natural structure and provide services relegated to social agencies elsewhere. Many churches are basically family groups. In fact, one of the difficulties of getting churches to work together is the fact that the families are separated by interests, character, or disagreements.

Although family loyalties are strong, individual members of the family seem to get along pretty much on their own. Few activities are planned to take place within the family. There is no strong sense of doing things together as a matter of planning and policy. Instead, the family seems to be held together by a sense of need for emotional support.

The closeness of the family in the mountains means that the family is more of a primary group in bringing up children than some other families. In a world of rapid change this has been detrimental because these families tend to be quite traditionalistic and thus "educate" their children to remain traditional. The family is so much a teaching unit for ideas about how life should be run and how the world really is that it has been difficult to reach youth with new ideas. There are some differences between the rural families and those who live in towns or coal camps. The static situation in the rural area where families have lived side by side for generations makes the family a basic unit for action, teaching, and socialization. As families moved into the coal camps they sought to adapt the family structures to this new environment. Therefore, the family was extended to include like-minded friends. Reference groups are usually divided on the basis of sex and age. These reference groups are composed of close kin and close neighbors and provide the social outlets, the comradeship, the action groups, and the community relationships. There is an interlocking membership in these groups so that each group knows what the others are thinking and doing. These are natural groupings that form as a step beyond the family group dependence structure (Weller, 1968).

Men have a tendency to belong more to the male reference group than they do to their own family. This is also true of women. Thus the family activities for men are found not with their wives and families but with a male group. There is a sharp role definition in the mountain culture; a man's work belongs to him alone and the woman's to her.

Babies are gladly welcomed in Appalachian familes. A small baby is a delight to all ages and is fondled, held, rocked, and spoiled in a grand style. Because he lives in the midst of the family it is not just the parents that do this but all the close kin.

Looff (1968) has commented that although the mountain infant is smothered with love by many persons, this changes as a child grows older. His interviews with families revealed that adults and older children freely gave themselves to the infants who seemed to thrive in every physical, emotional, and intellectual sense. However, beginning with the motor-muscular and pre-school stages of development there seems to be a considerable decrease in the amount of time given to the child. The young child is left on his own to grow up, develop, and learn as he wants to learn, without careful training or supervision. The mountain family tends to be adult-centered and it is what the adults in the family need, want, think and do that is important. Babies are like toys for adults to enjoy but they are to become little adults very quickly.

The over attentiveness given to the infant and withdrawn in later childhood leads to dependency on the family and brings about familialism. While a kind of informal control over children is exercised by the entire extended family, it lacks direct action and planning. This kind of parental non-attention and non-involvement in regard to their children may contribute to the basic insecurity and low self-image of the mountain people. As the mountain children grow up they tend to find direction in watching parents and other adults and modeling their behavior after them. This has some disadvantages. A variety of adult models is not available, and in many cases parents may not be the most successful models to emulate. The lack of adequate parental involvement with education and guidance of children tends to contribute to a pattern of dependency and does not motivate youths to drive toward achievement beyond what they are able to see.

Young people tend to marry early. Because the family is such an important element in the culture, youths think naturally in terms of forming their own. There is not the pressure to achieve goals that could force putting off marriage until a later date. If a girl stays in the region after her formal education, there is little for her to do except to get married. Jobs are not plentiful and most of them are not very rewarding. The adult models she has admired and been exposed to are almost exclusively those of wife and mother.

In choosing a mate there appears to be little free choice. The mate is chosen so that he will fit in with the family, but because this happens so naturally and informally it would probably be denied. When marriage occurs, the families of the bride and groom often are not involved in the ceremony. The couples go to a justice of the peace or to a preacher, frequently on the spur of the moment. During courtship and early marriage the reference group division by sex is broken down. Soon after marriage the old relationships pick up again, the husband with his friends and the wife with hers. As children begin to arrive, the wife assumes her domestic role. As the young parents become older they assume more recognition in the family and societal structure. Old people do not generally live with their children, but they do live close to them and the children make provision for them.

Another characteristic of the culture is its repressive nature. In a society where goals are not so achievable, life does not take on the attribute of driving toward goals. It tends, instead, to take on the character of living with that which is possible. If people are not able to acquire a new house or advance on the job, meaningful relationships with family and friends become more important. In many ways this relational society makes for a more peaceful and less competitive existence. Frequently, there is less sibling rivalry in the family structure than in a middle-class family. However, because one depends so much on family relationships he tends to be overconcerned with them. Life may be lived on a very shallow level, with disagreements quickly covered up and controversial issues avoided so that people will continue to get along. The great need to get along with the family does not expose family members to controversy and they do not learn how to handle it. This does not mean that it does not occur, but rather that when it does occur there are fewer attempts to learn to handle it. One of the disadvantages of the personalism in the mountain culture is that the people do not find it easy to work with others on an interpersonal basis (Weller, 1965a).

Religion

Like all other aspects of the Appalachian region, religion is a part of the great paradox. In this region the urban church — with its organization, class structure, and extensive volunteers — exists beside the mountain church with its lack of organization, volunteers, and class structure. However, the influence that seems to dominate is the ruralized mountain culture which stems from the past and has been refined and developed. This ruralized mountain culture affects the individual and his religious experience in many respects. Some of the general characteristics of religion in the Appalachian culture are outlined by

Nesius (1966): Christian beliefs are derived from a fundamentalist interpretation of the Bible so that to quote the Bible is to quote undisputable law; a knowledge of the exactness or correct reference to the Bible is very low — what the Bible says is learned from preachers and each preacher pursues his own philosophy; church membership in Appalachia is declining; religion has a very carefully circumscribed place — when the church begins to move in particular directions it oversteps its bounds; denominational rivalry and sectarianism are very keen. The mountain man does not become a Christian unless he is forced to and feels that he can back out of that commitment. His individualism and self-reliance remain intact through it all.

The first settlers in Appalachia were largely lower economic groups with diverse religious orientations. There were Scotch Presbyterians, Amish Puritans, Separatists, and non-conforming sectarians from various backgrounds (Brewer, 1962). No one church developed sufficient strength to draw all the people together. They were too widely separated and travel was too difficult for a stable ministry to be provided. Education of the clergy held no more appeal for the mountaineer than did any other education, so there grew up a group of lay preachers who were farmers or miners through the week and preachers on Sunday. When he "got religion" he felt the spirit. The preachers were plain folk who spoke in unlettered language.

The religious beliefs of the Appalachian mountaineer are closely related to his heritage and may be equated in a general way to the fundamentalist religious beliefs that prevail in the region today. "The evidence for this is found in the failure of Presbyterianism; the great revivals of the past; the revolt against symbolism, ecumenity, and the priesthood; the great Baptist movement; followership of Bishop Ashbury; the success of Holiness and Pentacostal groups; and the existence of many sect groups" (Nesius, 1966).

The Baptist form of government, which set up the local church as the only authority and allowed no interference from regional or national bodies, was most compatible with the philosophy of the mountaineer. The fierce individualism of the mountaineer carried this spirit to the extreme so that every man became his own highest authority (Caudill, 1963).

The church's characteristics include puritanical behavioral patterns, religious individualism, fundamentalism in attitudes toward the Bible and Christian doctrine, little distinction between clergy and laity, sectarian concepts of the church and its mission, revivalism, informality in public worship, and opposition to central authority of church and state (Brewer, 1962).

Caudill (1963) notes that the mountaineers are mainly irreligious and simply not joiners of organizations. In many areas the proportion of the church membership to population is below 30% with male participation somewhere around 5% and teenage membership falling to the range of 1–2%. It is not that mountain people are anti-religious. They talk a great deal about religion; it is one of their real life issues and religious arguments are a part of the standard talk in every reference group. But the extreme individualism of the mountaineer does not encourage him to participate in the church, much less to join it as a member. As in his relationship to the broader community, he does not understand the concept of church as a corporate community of believers. All churches are about the same and he could go to any of them. He wants to be able to sample revivals and services in order to find the one that meets his own needs. This approach leads to finding a church that satisfies his own ego. If the church does not suit him by what it is preaching by saying what he wants to hear and does not give him enough opportunity to assert himself to be heard, he may quit and go somewhere else. If he is strong enough, he may even form his own church. The mountaineer often turns to God only in times of crisis. Thus, religion represents a crutch for times of trouble, but it is not of much use in daily life. The mountaineer only appreciates the simple, literalistic interpretation of the Scriptures. An issue is either right or wrong, and people are impatient with the fine points or shades of meaning in between. To the mountaineer, the Bible is a magic book and he has a respectful reverence for it, but it is a reverence without scholarship. He may take passages out of context to suit his purpose or to reinforce his ideas.

The fundamentalist religious beliefs describe life on earth as a tragic drama. Eternal life is dependent upon predestination, redemption, and resistance to the temptations of Satan. Life should be full of trouble: suffering is viewed a period of testing to be offset by being saved. Those not saved must endure for all eternity the fiery torments of hell. Evangelistic preaching prevails and is aimed at instant conversions. Emotionalism is an important ingredient to the mountaineer religion. If the emotion which first moved him dies down or the crisis resolves itself, a person is prone to backslide. He simply gives up his faith, returns to his old ways, and is likely to blame it all on the devil. When temptations come again, he backslides, instead of using his faith to overcome them.

Fervent religious revivals have always been important in the region, and the custom continues today. Meetings are conducted in tents and bring excitement and action to the dull life of the mountaineer. Preaching is highly emotional, direct, and fear-filled as evangelists seek to convert sinners to a saving faith. Revival is still a major form of religious service in the mountains, emphasizing an emotional, episodic, and action-oriented kind of religious experience. A good revival service with a lively evangelist, enthusiastic singing and heart-rending special music, and a group prayer where all the faithful gather at the front and pray aloud at the same time can create an atmosphere of tense expectancy. Some of them "get happy" and begin "to speak with tongues." As the service provides release for people who have been pent up in the midst of their dull life, the explosions of emotions that occur in loud shouting and crying brings release to those who may not have other outlets.

The fatalism of the mountaineer leads him to the concept of other worldly and socially passive ethics. Because his hopes have been frustrated so often and because he has never lived with real joy, his eyes and heart have turned unto the promises of a future life. A study by Ford (1960) of one hundred Appalachian counties indicates that the fundamental religious beliefs are needed to prevail in the Appalachians. These beliefs were found to be stronger in the rural than the metropolitan or urban areas. They were also found to be stronger among the lower income and uneducated. This study suggested that as the urbanism advanced, a corresponding decline occurred in what is called the Puritan morality.

Kaplan (1965) studied the religious sentiments that appeared in southern Appalachia. He suggested that people use these sentiments as institutional or value systems to correct and cope with their environment. He studied the Free Will Baptist group in the mountains of western North Carolina during three summers, using the participant-observer method. He sought to identify sentiments in terms of what is, what ought to be, and what is desired and to analyse these sentiments in terms of their intensity, prevalence, influence, and impact on the processes of the group. Anyone working with a poverty group would miss a very strategic part of the system if he neglected the many and pervasive functions of their religion. Kaplan suggests that the sentiments of people such as those included in his study help fasten them in poverty. They had unstable jobs, small unproductive farms on the poorest land, poor housing, and they lacked education. Yet the sentiments did not encourage economic activity, but rather they emphasized that one's reward would be forthcoming in heaven. Other groups who share this particular religious value do encourage hard work in order to overcome economic hardships. It appears that religion for this group, with its sentiments about securing rewards in one's after-life, may act as a tension reducing device.

The group had strong feelings in regard to sex, which they equated with evil. The preachers constantly stated these sentiments in their sermons, and the evils of sex were a constant preoccupation of the members. Yet there was considerable sexual activity.

The dominant sentiment about expressing anger was of the variety, "Thou shalt not be angry." There was an emphasis that God was angry at them for their sinful thoughts and experiences, but it was unpardonable for them to be angry. They distrusted man's capacity for controlling his feelings which had to deal with sex and anger, often equating the two.

In regard to giving love, they felt that people could not be depended upon, and it was hard to love folks like that. Affective sentiments were directed toward Jesus as the Savior and the concept of love was defined as something you receive from Jesus, not something you give. They believed that they belonged to a fellowship of sufferers, rather than a religious group as a source of love. They were constantly told that they were unwanted and unloved by other people although loved by Jesus. They felt they were a fellowship of the damned.

To be saved meant to accept Jesus Christ as Lord and Savior. This is an act of faith; it is an emotional act which one feels deeply and to be saved is publicly stated and ritually confirmed. According to some religious groups to be saved means to be saved for all time for, although you may sin, you may never fall from grace; forgiveness is easily acquired. However, in the group that Kaplan studied, once saved did not mean always saved. Indeed the smallest sin may cause one to fall from the state of grace. People who could not remain saved were referred to as "Bible hardened." These were people who had been saved again and again but felt they could not remain free from sin and consequently gave up. According to the observations of this study, they gave up to withdrawal, alcoholism, and other asocial behavior. There was a great deal of concern about losing one's salvation, and as a result frequent revivals were held to allow one to become saved again and again.

The free expression of feelings in a rather uninhibited way was a characteristic of their church behavior. They had a very lively church atmosphere, conducive to yelling, wailing, crying and a talking in tongues. During the sermons the audience would participate in frequent and emphatic "amens." The sermons contained emotional outpourings, and the songs were sung with the fullest passion and frequently with tears. It appears reasonable to assume that they had a sentiment which allowed for expression of deep feelings in a spontaneous way.

Kaplan concluded that the sentiments of the group retarded rather than facilitated achievement. They were primarily adaptive retreats from successful coping. Deprived and beaten back as this particular group has been, they have few other institutional or value alternatives to correct or cope with their environment. This raises a key problem for those whose life is characterized by poverty: "How are more successful coping devices built into a way of life?"

Politics

The political aspect of the Appalachian resident's life is as much a paradox as other areas. One might reasonably assume, based upon the characteristics described earlier, that political activity would be an unimportant part of the mountain life. This is not at all the case. The Appalachian resident is interested and active in politics. This is probably due to the fact that those in power seem to reap large benefits from holding office. Some political offices are quite lucrative in terms of monetary reward as well as prestige.

Political office-seeking in many parts of Appalachia is an interesting phenomenon, but often incomprehensible to an outside observer. Campaigns, at least at local levels, are bitter with much name calling and personal attack. Since local areas are often enclaves of several large families, there is a family-type involvement in any political campaigning. The entire concept is based upon the politician's being able to make things better for himself and his supporters.

The tragic aspect of all this is that many other parts of life in Appalachia are tied to the power of the politician. Roads are built in the area served by the person in power to a greater extent than in other areas. Financial aid is given to schools and other social agencies on a ratio of political support more than any other factor. In addition, the educational system is often politically constituted. From the state level on down, the political persuasion of the office holder is often the key factor in support of educational endeavors. The incumbent may spend the final months of his tenure in a given position arranging the prospects for a new position he aspires to. This may not be much different from other states but the outcome in Appalachia is usually more noticeable.

Finally, this type of political activity tends to create long lasting rivalries with one group supporting certain projects only to have them deteriorate when another group gets into control. Thus, instead of some master plan for building and maintaining educational facilities the process sputters along depending upon the group presently in power. This leads to difficulties in establishing and using cooperative agencies for the provision of educational and personal service. Yet this is precisely what is necessary if the Appalachian area is to move forward in any positive way.

A further ramification of the political situation is seen in what happened to Appalachian land owners in their dealings with the coal mine owners. Many times, because the owner-operator also held political power, the landowner lost all rights to his property while at the same time he was the sole taxpayer on the property. Partly due to ignorance, but also due to a rather selfish attitude on the part of state and local law makers, land was literally destroyed in the search for coal with no attempt to restore or pay for the destroyed land. And at the end the land owner still was expected to pay tax on worthless land. Caudill (1963) tells of one farmer who sold the mineral rights from his land to one of the coal mines for fifty cents per acre. Millions of dollars worth of coal were mined from this property with no further compensation to the land owner and little new revenue paid by the enterprising coal miner to the state. The tragic aspect of this was that the farmer had had a thriving fruit farm with many trees producing an acceptable living income for him. The fifty cents per acre mineral rights included the right of the coal mine owner to get to the minerals any way possible. Since strip mining was the easiest and cheapest way the farmer lost his orchards and his livelihood and, when the coal was finally exhausted, had only non-productive land left.

It should come as no surprise that the resident in Appalachia has suspicion for those who come to "help" him. He has experienced many previous "helps" and found that those cost him dearly. He also has translated this reaction into a policy of "get what you can from whomever you can because the other guy is just waiting to take you." A combination of factors have led the Appalachian resident to a distrust of outsiders, to a rather non-motivated life, and to an attitude of fairly selfish indulgence in his own immediate needs. He has lost so much in his dealing with outsiders that he no longer can trust anyone. This attitude is transferred early to the children of Appalachia and interferes with normal educational pursuits.

2

Education and Work

Appalachian Schools

Schools in this area of the nation, like all American schools, are a direct reflection of the social-political-economic structure of the society which creates and maintains them. To understand the Appalachian schools, one might well direct his attention to the social system of which they are an integral part. Recall that Weller (1965) described the people as being highly individualistic, oriented toward tradition, fatalistic, seekers of action, and person-oriented. The schools are products of and contributors to the social system established by such values.

Sociological literature classifies social systems as open or closed; hence, schools and school systems can be examined as open or closed to innovations in instructing society's youth. The educational systems and the schools in much of Appalachia have in the past been predominantly closed just as the larger social system of which they are a part. The general characteristics of the people and their subsequent social-political structure accompanied by severe restrictive economic conditions have inhibited progress toward openness.

Ogletree (1968) describes some of the characteristics of Appalachian schools. Although his descriptions were validated by widespread positive reactions from colleagues in Appalachia, it is recognized that it is dangerous to generalize about the entire region. The children in

Appalachia have been physically and psychologically isolated from the type of normal educational and cultural opportunities available to most children. Although every child has the opportunity to attend public schools, schools vary from the one-room type to the modern centralized system. Long bus rides are often necessary. Nonetheless, few children do not have the possibility of twelve years of public school. Because the forms of education were imposed from the outside and did not grow up as an expression of the culture there has traditionally been a resistance to book learning.

Communities are culturally deprived and the homes of many youngsters are devoid of educational material typically associated with the American home. Although the children are of normal intelligence, social and cultural isolation limits their ability to respond to many standardized culturally contaminated tasks. The child's low evaluation of life's opportunities is also related to the environment. He sees life in the community as his world and often sees little relationship between schooling and the good life. Education must have immediate and specific application for the people to feel that it is important or necessary. Yet most schools have taught and still teach standard college preparatory courses. The education presented to the mountaineer is the kind of education that he does not understand, and it presents ideals he does not share. Although the mountaineer is not interested in abstract ideas or the intellectual fine points or learning for learning's sake, this is the normal activity which faces the student as he enters school.

Schools are accepted as an established part of the tradition and their role tends to be strongly conditioned by local history. "The tried and true are good enough." The low community expectations of schools are further illustrated by the low level of financial support afforded them, and consequently salaries and per pupil expenditures are usually low in these districts. Parents want their children to have an education because they have become increasingly aware that it is necessary. However, they fear that it will separate the childern from their families and destroy the common level of reference group.

Most of the professional personnel are indigenous to the district within which they are employed and have attended colleges or universities close to their homes. Those who are not tend to be married to local people or are natives of nearby counties. In fact, many school boards specifically give preference to local personnel over outside applicants. Nepotism is often a way of life and the institutionalization of the mores and attitudes of the family are presented anew in the offerings of the school. As one might guess, the criteria for selecting teachers tend toward saving money or keeping the wealth within the family rather than toward acquiring qualified and adequately trained personnel. Therefore, the school personnel are consistent with their culture and oftentimes tend to place local customs and values above their professional judgments.

Many school districts have found it neither necessary nor desirable to operate with written school board policies or procedures. Schools are informally organized and operated. Most of the schools are operated on the thesis of hire a teacher, assign him to a school, give him his books and let him teach. Little attention or effort is made to fit the instructional program to the social-economic needs of the students. The instructional program is frequently that of teachers and textbooks with only the teacher deciding what to teach and when.

Like most teachers, school administrators are natives of the districts in which they are employed and are place- rather than career-oriented in their profession. Their conversations with each other tend to be on personal matters rather than on professional matters. Administrators are also people-oriented and seem only concerned that teachers' behaviors result in no problems or criticisms. Many administrators personally operate the school stores, plan lunchroom menus, and even purchase the food. They have to purchase their own supplies, coal, lights, and telephone from funds raised by the school rather than furnished by the school board. The reader may wish to examine some of the writing of Jesse Stuart to get a picture of the type of situation which the Appalachian teacher may face. He will also find that dedicated people, such as Stuart, can make school and education a meaningful experience in the lives of students.

The Changing Scene

Many observers believe the schools in Appalachia have undergone great change in the last ten years. Recent Federal legislation has had an impact on the total social-economic structure. The schools within this larger social system have therefore changed. Social change has been far greater than many people thought possible in such a brief period. Others argue that the process is changing too slowly, that educational change is dropping even further behind changes in other sectors of the society. Regardless of the issues being debated, the fact remains that Federal legislation is resulting in alterations in the educational systems in Appalachia.

The advent of the Elementary and Secondary Education Act of 1965 served as an external stimulus to the system and resulted in considerable challenge to the status quo equilibrium of the educational system. Higher education and particularly local schools have felt the impact of this legislation. The allocation of funds was not automatic. School districts had to follow an established procedure requiring that applications be based on an analysis of needs, that proposed activity be logically related to the reduction of those needs, that the operating procedures clearly indicate their appropriateness to the proposed program and that evaluation of the procedures be conducted. For the first time many schools were asked to plan. They were asked to develop a program predicted to achieve specified goals and to determine the extent to which these goals were achieved. Such a procedure had been totally foreign to many schools and many educators (Ogletree, 1968). Parenthetically, many districts did not receive funds because no one was able to deal either with writing a proposal or with finding the necessary assistance to fulfill the stated criteria.

Accommodations to this external intervention were achieved in many ways and in various school systems. Many districts felt compelled to take advantage of the funds made available and moved rapidly in order to benefit during the first year. They have kept moving ever since. The typical method of adjustment to meet these external requirements has been the creation of a somewhat separate school program, one which could be removed if Federal funds were curtailed. This type of adjustment permits a local district to operate its basic program much as it did prior to 1965. However, the involvement of school personnel in planning, implementing, and evaluating has and will continue to upset the status quo and should give impetus to more basic and lasting changes.

The entire Appalachian region appears to be suffering from a professional manpower shortage because of the initiation of many new programs. Regular classroom teachers have been assigned to the new programs, creating vacancies which are difficult to fill. The insular pattern has been maintained by the avoidance of employing staff from outside the district who might inject new perceptions into the system. This pattern seems to be shifting. As the programs continue, an increasing number of schools seem to be recruiting personnel from outside the area on the basis of ability. The gradual breaking down of provincialism has increased communication within school districts, between districts, and among districts, the state, and Federal agencies. Districts are becoming proud of what they are able to do, and some are being recognized for their innovativeness and for the effectiveness of their programs. A portion of the legislation designed for innovation and demonstration projects and supplementary centers has been capitalized upon to develop multi-county or regional programs. It is hoped that this movement will stimulate progress and reduce provincialism.

In light of these conditions, it is apparent that schools are improving so that quality education for the children of Appalachia is possible today. Although it may be less adequate in this region than other sections of the country, conditions are quite unlike those of a few years ago.

Work

Work has never been particularly enjoyable for the Appalachian—it has been a necessity. He had not planned to enter a particular occupation because he liked it, but he worked at whatever there was to do because he had to make a living. Therefore, the concept of choosing a vocation and becoming trained in that field was not part of his education. The idea that people can actually enjoy work or that it has a creative outlet and provides fulfillment makes little sense to him. One works to live.

Because work is viewed as only a way to earn a living, and because there is much unemployment, the Appalachian has an attitude toward unemployment insurance different from the middle class leaders who set up such payments. Such insurance was originally conceived as temporary assistance between jobs. However, many Appalachians see this insurance as a legal substitute for work for the entire period that it comes to them. Since all you work for is money and since you can get money legally when you are not working, why work! (Weller, 1965b)

The Appalachian kind of cultural arrangement was satisfactory enough for the isolated, agrarian, independent life of the mountains in the past, but it is simply not adequate for making a living in the technological world of today. The Appalachian has lived in a "closed door" society that denied him a chance for advancement, wealth, or achievement. This is in contrast to the overall American "open door" society of almost limitless opportunity.

There has been little interest for a person to achieve outside goals. A man strives toward being accepted as a person within a group. Whatever goals he does achieve are won in relation to other persons and are a product of participation in a group. This person-orientation has several ramifications: he does not make long-range plans for his life; he is not a doer, and he finds relationships with people to be primary. He is suspicious of doctors, social workers, and government people because they treat him in impersonal ways. If he moves to a city he finds that people there treat him impersonally and he regards it as hostile.

In accordance with his view, the mountaineer brings up his child to be sensitively aware of persons and relationships. A negative result of this personal orientation is the hostility that it creates toward leadership. Persons who seek to rise above the reference group immediately become suspect and the leader may find himself cut off from the group in which he has found his basic security.

Mangalam (1965) reported a study illustrating the value system in which family and kin were more important than work. This is considerably different from the general society with its emphasis on work, achievement, and success. He also reported that even though there were not sufficient opportunities, the large majority of people was not willing to move.

Many workers do migrate to other locations. We do not know if they have higher aspirations or in what ways they are affected by the new environment. It is apparent that high school students of families who migrated from Appalachia have higher vocational aspirations than those who remain in Appalachia. Stevic and Uhlig (1967) reported that migrant youths had different personal role models and characteristics for success than youths who remained in Appalachia. The migrant youths perceived effort and commitment as much more important for success. One problem for the Appalachian youth seems to be the limited number of role models and the lack of information available. Presumably, a program of educational and vocational guidance is needed to stimulate and assist the youth of Appalachia.

Migration

One may view migrants as belonging to two main classes: those who are "pushed out" by the lack of opportunity, and those who are "pulled out" by greater attractions elsewhere. Job opportunities and cities act as a large pull factor whereas the lack of opportunities in the rural area operates as a push factor. The interplay between push and pull is undoubtedly a function not only of unemployment but of such factors as population size, composition and functional base as well. Reasons for moving may be thought of by the migrant either in terms of the qualities or circumstances of the present location or those of the potential location. The vast majority of migration occurs from a combination of push-pull factors; for example, a lack of employment in one place and kin relations in another, may combine to encourage migration for the purpose of seeking employment (Schweiker, 1968).

Employment services for people are provided by close kin. People are far more inclined to move to places where kin are located and are more apt to respond to a kinsman's word that there are jobs available than they are to the advice of employment agencies. Families located in a city provide job information for those back home and then provide a home for the migrant when he arrives and assist in his adjusting to the city. This kind of orientation is not what most cities prefer because the ghetto areas are extended and migrants pile into overcrowded housing. Still the kin relationship has made a tremendous contribution by providing security and information to the migrant when he first arrives. After this initial phase the system breaks down. The natural "back home" system is broken up because not everybody moves, and the migrant finds himself in an alien society with no resources to cope with it effectively. The concept of rugged individualism and primary reliance on family in overcoming life's troubles make it very difficult for the Appalachian to adjust to urban society where the close-knit family structure is disabling since the things it was designed to combat no longer exist.

More than 2 million southern Appalachians have migrated to northern cities since World War II and they are still coming to join relatives in a world where they are seldom understood and often feared. In 1966 Chicago was reported to have an estimated 40,000 Appalachians who had formed a ghetto in the uptown section not far from Lake Michigan (Ernst, 1966). Others concentrated around cities which permitted them to commute home quite easily.

Money is not really important to the Appalachian migrants; all they want is enough to live on. When they earn as much as they did in Appalachia, plus enough to compensate for the higher cost of living, they frequently quit until the following week. Education is primarily looked upon in America as the best way to get a better paying job. But Appalachian migrants do not consider work to be the fundamental purpose of their lives. Therefore, it is not surprising that the typical male migrant drops out of school after the sixth grade. Their attitude toward work and money tends to freeze them in the ghetto and encourages a desperate commuting between Appalachia, where many of them continue to own homes, and the large city during hard times. Appalachian disdain for community action, that is, working with others beyond their families to achieve common goals, deprives them of any political muscle which may help ease their plight in the city. The Appalachian is repelled by the neighborhood center and other agencies with their bureaucratic procedure. He detests the rows of desks, the long forms to be filled out, prying personal questions, delays that result in only inadequate aid, being treated as a case instead of a person, the failure to consider his problems as he sees them. Agencies undoubtedly do some good, but their bureaucratic procedures and their apparent failure to hire enough people who know how to work with Appalachian migrants keep them from reaching the mass of these migrants (Ernst, 1966).

The process of adapting to an industrial work situation encountered in migration may be one of the more serious sources of stress in the adjustment from rural to urban life. The individual has little opportunity prior to migration to acquire industrial work experiences. Upon arrival he seeks out and assumes the work role for which he has had very little, if any, preparation. Appalachian migrants frequently settle in urban or suburban communities in or near the centers of industry which are populated for the most part by similar migrants.

Migrants frequently move with the accompanying knowledge that many before them, usually kinfolk and neighbors, have been successful in making the transition and adapting to the industrial work situation. Dependency of the migrant is usually tied in with the supportive functions performed by the kinship structure. From significant kin group members in the area of destination the migrant gets information about the kinds of jobs available as well as some idea about work expectations connected with the industrial occupation. In numerous ways the transition from field to factory in the process of adaptation to industrial work situations is usually begun long before the migrant leaves Appalachia.

Employers not only recognize the importance of kinship ties among the mountaineers but utilize the migrant kin network to secure an adequate labor supply especially at the laborer and unskilled job levels. When vacancies occur the word gets passed along within the shop and via the kin communication network and it soon becomes common knowledge in the migrant community. The word goes back to families in the hollows of Appalachia. Such personal appeals continue to be more effective than mass media in drawing job applicants from the mountain labor pool. The proximity to Appalachia which allows the migrant to maintain visiting ties with his family through supportive kin who work in the area are the main determinants in the migration pattern.

The Appalachian migrant is rather reluctant to change jobs because it not only entails moving into an unfamiliar situation but also means that he must give up the security of his seniority rights. Some, of course, are encouraged to rise up through the ranks within the factory where they had started, and seniority rules and the factors tied in with the particular firm's organization of manpower affect this. To capitalize on their experience, upward movement toward higher paying and more skilled jobs frequently means seeking out new employers. Although they may secure their initial job through the aid and influence of kin, those who subsequently change jobs are more likely to do so on their own.

The threat of being laid off is an ever present fact in the life of manual workers. In general, the Appalachian accepts the threat of a layoff as one of those annoying conditions of industrial work like punching a time clock and working indoors. With seniority on a job the threat is reduced. During a layoff period, most try to make the best of it by drawing unemployment compensation, or they attempt to find other jobs and wait for their old jobs to re-open.

A case study of the adjustment of the Appalachian migrants to the industrial society reports that over the years they were able to make a satisfactory transition from the field to the factory (Schwarzweller, 1969). The record of upward occupational mobility in the urban area was regarded as impressive under the circumstances, and a relatively long tenure in current jobs was regarded as a sign of stability, acceptance of the industrial work role, and successful adaptation to the industrial work situation. When interviewed regarding job satisfactions, most of the informants emphasized they liked the kind of work they were doing because it was interesting or they were learning something different. They talked a lot about the working conditions, such as whether or not it was a clean job or they were working with a nice crew. The amount of take-home pay and the degree of security were important conditions. The interpersonal relationships among the work crew members and the boss were of prime importance (Schwarzweller, 1969).

In another study, Riccio (1965) reported that students of Appalachian migrant families who settled in a lower middle-class community did not differ significantly in terms of their occupational aspirations, role models, or cultural conformity from non-migrant students. He concluded that the adolescent who moved from Appalachia could not be viewed in stereotypic fashion because of his geographical origin.

Professional personnel also migrate. Because Appalachian teachers' salaries are low, there is a flow of teachers to better paying districts in eastern and northern states. Typically the Appalachian teachers locate geographically so that weekend trips home can be made conveniently. Many leave their families in Appalachia, rent a room in the new district, and commute home on weekends and holidays. They tend to feel more secure in districts that employ teachers from areas near their home. Their social life then is restricted to activities among the members of that group. The members of the group as a whole seem to adjust remarkably well, although there are exceptions where new candidates simply cannot adjust to the new environment. Often, new arrivals bring with them speech characteristics of their geographic area. If the teacher has a heavy accent, communication problems may result. Students and parents occasionally experience difficulty in understanding some of the teachers. However, teacher turnover rate among relocated Appalachian teachers is low. After the initial move and adjustment to it they are likely to remain. A second move to a different school would require moving farther away from home and would also involve the risk of adjusting to another new group of people and perhaps a new set of values (Mayer, 1966).

Two mobility demonstration projects conducted in Appalachia (1967) by state employment services reported that there was no lack of persons willing to move, but that millions of those who relocated were not prepared to adjust to town or city life and about half of those who moved away came home within six months to a year. Many had received MDTA training, but skilled training alone was not enough to cope with the transition from the mountains to the metropolis. This finding suggests that there is no program for the social man or the psychological man to go with the economic man (Zeller, 1967).

Counselors in communities populated by migrants from Appalachia can help students adjust to a new school and way of life. A knowledge of their cultural background may assist counselors in individualizing the guidance assistance.

3

Organization of Guidance Services

General Guidance Organization

There are several methods of organizing guidance services which may be applicable to the Appalachian schools. In this portion of the monograph we shall present general programs. Later we shall attempt to speak specifically to guidance needs in Appalachia.

Truax (1956) has suggested that one can conceive of guidance services as dealing in several areas of need in the school. In general, he suggests that the guidance program and thus the counselor ought to be concerned with providing the following services.

Services to Individual Students

This category would include many of the traditional activities subsumed under presently functioning programs. Individual assistance in the form of advising and counseling on vocational, educational, and personal matters would constitute the bulk of the counselors' activities in this area.

Services to Students in Groups

Again this is an area that is somewhat traditionally included in many guidance programs. The research tends to suggest that most of the activity in this area is oriented toward guidance rather than counseling. Thus, guidance-oriented group activities are often designed to teach the students, rather than group counseling activities which deal with more personal topics and could be student-initiated. Goldman's classification (1962) describes this very effectively when he lists nine levels which might constitute the continuum of group processes. At one extreme we find the usual subject matter classroom groups in which the leader plans the topics with emphasis on facts and skills, while at the opposite end we find those groups formed to meet the needs of members in which feelings are emphasized and the topics are more closely related to nonschool orientation.

Establishing and Maintaining Staff Relationships

In this area the activities of the counselor are directed toward the understanding and involvement of the school staff in guidance tasks. In addition to the informational activities, i.e., what the counselor is attempting to do, he would be concerned with including the staff in planning, implementing, and evaluating guidance services. Where appropriate they would also be included in the provision of services.

Establishing and Maintaining Community Relationships

The involvement of the counselor in this aspect of guidance includes several areas. First, community resource personnel who could assist the student should be identified. A second aspect is the involvement of the community in planning and implementing school and guidance programs. This becomes especially important in areas such as Appalachia where a portion of the educational problem can be traced to parental and community apathy. Third, there is a need to identify employment and educational potential in the community and to devise ways in which these can be most effectively used. Again, in Appalachia this may be a very crucial task in that the potential for the immediate community may be limited. This further suggests that the counselor should extend his survey beyond the immediate community.

Promoting the General School Program

Although he is not a curriculum expert, the counselor should be acquainted with academic needs of the pupils in his school. By conducting follow-up studies, by action research, by working closely with a large number of students, or by any of several other sources, the counselor can obtain this information and help in translating it into meaningful curriculum programs.

Accepting Professional Responsibilities

The final aspect of the counselor's role in a fully functioning guidance program deals with his own professional growth. He needs to be involved in various professional organizations for two purposes. First, it will provide a vehicle for his continued growth as a professional counselor and promote initiation and continued improvement of meaningful guidance activities. Second, it provides an opportunity for the counselor to share with other professionals. This may include such activities as supervision of counseling, sharing of programs to be tested in other settings, evaluation of function, and establishing of a base for continuation of the growth of school counseling as a profession.

The American School Counselors' Association (ASCA) policy statement (1965) specified the following functions for inclusion in a guidance program.

Planning and Development of the Program

In all too many cases the programmatic aspects of guidance are neglected. It is either assumed that a program already exists and the problem is one of fitting in or that there are too many other tasks to perform. When one deals with any unique situation such as Appalachia he must be concerned with defining objectives, identifying needs and developing plans of action and evaluation. This is necessary since guidance programs in Appalachia have not been particularly successful in providing for the needs of youth and a new approach is essential.

Counseling

The central portion of most guidance programs is counseling. The counselor helps the individual to understand and accept himself and he provides opportunities for the student to obtain personal and environmental information. In short, in the one-to-one setting the counselor provides an opportunity for the student to examine his personal needs, to ascertain the availability of alternatives, to move toward and make decisions, and to evaluate his behavior in a non-threatening environment.

Pupil Appraisal

The guidance specialist provides leadership in the accumulation of meaningful information for each student. Some thought should be given to the process necessary to accomplish this and in addition to the clerical involvement demanded. The counselor coordinates the esstablishment and maintenance of confidential files. He interprets the information for the student and others who have a right to it in order to assist the student in his decisions.

Educational and Occupational Planning

One of the tasks in which the counselor is engaged is related to the educational and occupational informational needs of students. Traditionally, class scheduling has been a part of the counselor's role with the general assumption that this is educational planning. It may be, but often the process is a mechanical administrative task with little or no attempt to describe what various courses and sequences of courses contain or how these might relate to future academic or occupational goals. In a similar vein we may make occupational information available, but the process of using, understanding, and applying the knowledge is left to the student to decipher. In general, the counselor needs to provide sufficient time for the counselee to examine information, to understand himself, and to integrate these two factors most appropriately into a course of action. In recent years several mechanical methods have been devised that allow the student to investigate several career areas and to obtain a prediction of success based upon personal factors compared with the characteristics of the occupation under consideration. These methods help, but eventually the student must choose, and the counselor can have important input into the final decision.

Referral

The counselor should be knowledgeable about various agencies, services, and persons which provide specialized assistance. Within the school and community many such sources exist and should when appropriate supplement the school's activities.

Placement

In this area the counselor is called upon to assist the student in finding the most appropriate placement in educational and occupational areas. This applies to placement in classes and programs within school, as well as post-school placement, i.e., college and job entry. The counselor needs to avoid mechanizing this process because it is still the prerogative and responsibility of the student to decide and to move into those areas chosen.

Parent Help

The school has traditionally attempted to involve parents in its operation, but in many cases these attempts have not succeeded because they have not been meaningful to the parent. Parent-teacher conferences and associations often do not live up to expectations because of the inability of both parents and teachers to fully utilize the potential. The counselor ought to be a leader in providing meaningful assistance and information to parents. In addition, the counselor can develop ways of improving the teaching staff's skill in this area since the involvement and motivation of parents are essential, especially in Appalachia.

Staff Consultation

Following the above direction the counselor can be helpful to teachers in a variety of areas. He can aid in the identification of students with special needs. He can provide liaison assistance between teacher and various people. He can suggest ways by which the teacher can more clearly relate his activities to the needs of students. The counselor may be forced to clearly delineate his activities with teachers in order to maintain a consultative stance as opposed to being a counselor to teachers. However, consultation can be a fruitful area for counselor involvement.

Local Research

The need to understand the local and regional situation is especially pressing in Appalachia. There is a need to determine what the community is like, what opportunities exist, what the characteristics of the student population are and what school leavers do. This is a much neglected portion of most counselors' functions, but it is especially important when such unique needs and situations exist as in Appalachia.

Public Relations

In an area where education is not seen as an extremely important aspect of one's life, community relations and community involvement are essential. It is probably safe to assume that the old adage of a good program selling itself is no longer viable. The school staff, including the counselor, should accept public relations as part of their responsibilities. This suggests that counselors inform people about the direction and activities of the program. Community understanding leads to greater community support of programs. And in Appalachia, one of the pressing needs is support of education by the community.

The statements above contain an outline for the creation, implementation, and continuation of guidance programs. Not every part can always be included in the program provided in schools. Lack of facilities, money, and personnel often preclude this. In addition the needs of the particular school should be related to the program. What these outlines provide is a framework on which to develop programs, to determine priorities, and to evaluate outcomes.

A guidance program must be predicated upon a foundation that allows for evaluation, for understanding, and for revision when necessary. The structure suggested above fulfills this requirement and offers the counselor an opportunity to implement services which provide for student, school, and personal needs. Obviously, a hierarchy will be established since it is generally impossible to provide each of these to the fullest extent except in ideal situations. This type of situation does not often exist in Appalachia. The counselor needs to spend some effort and time in acquiring basic information such as the characteristics of the school, the students, and the community.

Strategies for Guidance

Regardless of the goals or objectives which one establishes for a guidance program, there need to be strategies for achieving these goals. Stewart and Warnath (1965) describe three such strategies which have relevance to the attainment of these goals. They identify remedial, preventive, and promotional strategies.

In the remedial strategy the general behavior is to apply some solution to a problem or weakness after it has been identified. During 1958 and 1959 there was concern over the fact that mathematicians and scientists were not being developed in sufficient numbers to keep ahead of others in technological endeavors. The strategy at that time was to apply massive remediation in the form of monetary support for counseling in the schools and tests and measures. In so doing our efforts were directed at one portion of the population. This population was helped, but other populations needing remediation began to appear. Efforts are often spent in massive attempts to remediate certain behaviors which may have gone too far for successful remediation.

The preventive strategy builds upon the notion that we know that certain present behaviors have an effect upon the future or that there is a developmental progression to both positive and negative behaviors. Prevention is related to the provision of service or assistance prior to the actual onset of some behavior with the general notion that in so doing undesirable behavior or patterns of behavior will be avoided.

The final strategy is that of promoting those skills, attitudes, and habits necessary for a fully functioning individual. Included in this strategy is the issue of individual versus society. Can the individual make decisions or move in directions that are self-enhancing but antisocial? To whom or to what does the counselor owe primary allegiance?

It is clear that both the individual and society must be considered and that the counselor must be aware of their interaction and the potential problems which this issue may lead to. The individual student must ultimately take responsibility for his life and accept the consequences of actions whether positive or negative. The counselor's involvement is to insure that the environment where these decisions can take place exists. He needs to aid the student in examining his strengths, weaknesses, aptitudes, interests, and the societal structure in which he lives. The counselor may be called upon to help alter the social environment so that the promotion of the optimum development of the student can proceed.

In summary, each of the above strategies has merit. Obviously there are many times in the school life of young adults that remediation is essential. This must be provided for. In too many instances the number of such problems and the lack of personnel preclude going any further than remediation. Prevention is an equally important part of the job of the counselor as well as that of other school personnel. Guidance in the elementary school is one example of prevention in action. If we can aid students to make progress in academic and personal growth in the elementary school, the chances for problems later in life are greatly diminished. Finally, the promotional strategy should have the highest priority when choice is possible. Promoting positive actions and attitudes, and providing opportunities for the examination of self and the world — in short, establishing those conditions which promote rather than inhibit growth — hold forth the greatest hope for meaningful development of the potentials of all students.

In terms of Appalachia, it is apparent that for a period of time the remedial strategy will take precedence. The amelioration of student concerns or problems will be a primary task of the counselor. Lack of motivation, inadequate self-perception, and the everyday crises associated with being a resident and student in Appalachia suggest that remediation is most appropriate.

However, it is essential that the counseling and teaching staff include preventive assistance for the student. As suggested earlier, the inclusion of guidance at the elementary level is a feature of preventive strategy. Assistance offered junior and senior high students should also attempt to prevent school leaving, to present adequate educational and vocational information, and to develop decision-making skills. The student needs to become aware of the relationship between present functioning and future opportunities. He needs to understand that he has some control over his present and future life and to be encouraged to exert this control. Thus, the counselor can provide some preventive assistance to the Appalachian student by involving him in the process of self-examination as related to the development of vocational skills, educational opportunities and decision-making.

The promotional strategy in Appalachia will probably need to be delayed for a while. The immediate needs of the students will demand immediate action of a remedial and preventive nature. However, it will be of value to begin to program in those activities that are characteristic of the promotional strategy. These tasks include providing assistance at various points in the student's life based upon the understanding of development and of the uniqueness of the student. The student needs to have the opportunity to continually reassess his own strengths and weaknesses as well as the structure of the various societies or groups of which he is a member. In Appalachia this means that the student will be aided from early in his school career to deal realistically with himself as well as the rather repressive society.

Current ideas about guidance include the need to develop a longitudinal approach on a K–12 basis. Thus, it is essential to deal with the provision of guidance at several levels and to integrate the activities at each level as closely as possible. There are important differences which must be taken into account at each of the levels. There are also similarities or developmental aspects which need to be considered regardless of school level.

Elementary Level

Guidance at the elementary level is aimed at providing developmental or preventive guidance for students. Although individual counseling is an important part of the specialist role, there are other functions that deserve equal attention. Consultation with teachers and parents is of extreme importance for the elementary specialist. In addition, the specialist is often called upon for coordination of the variety of services available within the school and the community. In addition, there are several unique facets within the various services which need to be included in the preparation and functioning of the elementary guidance specialist.

Counseling

That counseling is the central function of the guidance worker's role remains true at the elementary level. The specialist is called upon to provide individualized assistance to the student. Since he is operating at the elementary level, the degree of seriousness of problems or concerns is less than at a higher level. Thus, there seems to be greater potential for aiding in the resolution of the concern. However, it is also apparent that the communications skills of the elementary child demand higher competency on the part of the guidance specialist. He may need to utilize various methods to move toward communication. Such methods as play media are valuable adjuncts for the specialist, but these methods demand specialized preparation and supervision.

A second limitation that exists at all levels but is perhaps more severe at the elementary level is related to the freedom of movement and choice which the elementary student has. The specialist must deal with this aspect as he works in a counseling relationship with the student. He must know the limits, the freedom—in short, the environments—in which the student moves, in order to provide effective assistance to the student.

Consultation

The elementary counselor will be called upon to provide consultative assistance to several groups within and outside the school. This process is differentiated from counseling in that the focus of attention is a person or problem outside the immediate environment. A teacher may need assistance on gaining a clearer understanding of the causes of and possible solutions for the behavior of a child in her class. The guidance specialist, as well as other specialists, meets with the teacher and provides assistance in the resolution of the concern. This type of consultative assistance constitutes an important part of the elementary guidance specialist's activities.

The specialist is also in an advantageous position to provide consultative assistance to parents. At the elementary school level, parents tend to show more interest in the activities of the school and their child's relationship to the school. However, this type of activity demands a special kind of involvement and perhaps training so that the parents can be aided in their attempts to provide a more meaningful social and psychological environment for the child.

The counselor may be called upon to provide consultative service to others within the school and community situation, e.g., administrative personnel. He should see this as an important part of his position and be prepared to spend the time and effort necessary to promote an effective learning and living situation for the student.

Coordination

A third task area for the elementary counselor is that of coordination. He will be called upon to bring various school personnel and other people together to provide more meaningful assistance to students. Depending of course upon the personnel available, the elementary guidance specialist may be called upon to contact such persons as school social workers, teachers, school psychologists, and community people such as agency personnel. The general expectation is that these people will be able to provide more meaningful assistance through cooperative activities. There is also a need to avoid an overlap of services. The elementary person is the most appropriate person in most cases since he has the time necessary for coordination and also, among the non-teaching specialists, he is most closely associated with one school.

In summary, the guidance specialist at the elementary level has three major functions that contribute to the educational experience of the child: counseling, consultation and coordination.

Intermediate Level

At present there is a minor trend to change the organizational structure of the school away from the common K–6, 7–9, 10–12 arrangement to several other arrangements. The aspect of this change that is of most importance to the present discussion concerns the change from a junior high school (7–9) to a middle school which might include grades 5–9 or any of several combinations thereof. In this discussion of appropriate services to be offered at various levels, we shall be dealing with the needs of students in the age range of about 11–14 regardless of the structure of the school which they attend.

When the student reaches the age level 11–14 we can expect certain needs to begin which relate to the transition from childhood to adulthood, to educational and vocational awakenings, to personal and social maturation, and to the very non-static orientation of the student. In order to meet these needs the school must be prepared to provide several types of services for each student.

First, in the area of personal social guidance, the intermediate student needs to have opportunities for meaningful interaction with other students, both of the same and of the opposite sex. In addition, this is a crucial period of time for relationships with adults, especially parents, and there is a need to promote communication in this area. The school counselor must be prepared to offer this type of interaction. Group discussions, individual conferences, parent-child-teacher-counselor conferences become important tools for the counselor's use.

The 11–14 year old student is beginning to see beyond the immediacy of the day to his future. He sees more clearly the relationship that exists between what he is doing now and possibilities for the future. He senses that he must begin, at this point in his life, to deal with his own life and how he wishes to order this life. Obviously, he also is faced with conflicting pressures from parents, teachers, other adults, and his peer group which range from rather subtle to very strong. In the midst of this the student is expected to maintain a delicate balance. He is expected to "act" adult but he does not yet have the physical ability to engage in some of the activities. He is expected to select those aspects of the lives of adults which are "right" and to reject those which are "wrong." And, although he may not have guidelines for this selection, he is told when he has not selected properly.

In terms of educational planning and decision-making, the 11–14 year old is expected, in many cases for the first time in his life, to select courses and to make educational decisions for himself. He is also issued, in all too many cases, a not too thinly veiled threat that if he does not choose accurately he will be sorry about it. The school counselor must provide meaningful assistance to the student in this case. It is often of considerable value to include the parents in any educational discussion since they are involved in the decision-making either directly or indirectly and, perhaps more importantly, can help the student ultimately to work through and implement his decision.

It is at this point in time that curricular understanding by the counselor is important in order to promote effective decision-making information for the student in terms of his understanding of himself and of present and future educational opportunities. The type of educational counseling which the counselor provides at the intermediate level will affect much of the future educational goals which the student sets and to which he commits himself.

Vocational guidance at this level is also of considerable importance. It is to be hoped of course, that some previous effort has been made at the elementary level. However, since elementary school guidance as a widespread phenomenon is not the case at the beginning of the 1970 decade, the first exposure that many students will have to vocational guidance will be at the intermediate level. Without going deeply into the nature of vocational development theory, it should be noted that vocational development and some maturation of choice is an important process to be accomplished during this period. Information is essential and the concepts of self understanding and understanding of the world of work become relevant. Some meaningful vocational activities should be built into the school activities of the intermediate student. In short, there is a need to provide opportunities for the student to examine his own attributes and to relate these to the general area of vocations and/or occupations.

The reader is cautioned against the assumption that the activities described above can be as neatly separated as suggested. These areas are overlapping and the counselor is often confronted with the student who ostensibly is involved in a "simple" educational decision which, in reality, is included in problems of identity, parental relationships, alienation, and peer group pressurization. It should be further noted that the intermediate level is the point at which many educational decisions become "final." School dropouts quite often make the final decision during this period. The educational attainment level is often crystallized, realistically or unrealistically, at this time.

High School Level

The high school counselor is called upon to help the student decide many of his educational or vocational choices. And as he needs to provide services similar to those offered at the previous level, he must offer the student assistance in the implementation of the decision. Perhaps an example will illustrate the point.

Let us assume that during the preceding periods of time, student A had been helped to successfully design a curricular program which prepared him with relative ease to matriculate at a college of his choice. He must now begin to finalize the several decisions involved in the transistion from high school to college. Is he going to go to college becomes one question. If he is, what are his interests, what would he like to do in life, what does he know about college, what is necessary to apply, be accepted, and attend college? These and a multitude of other questions must be answered before a meaningful choice can be made. The counselor must be involved in this process. He must go beyond the general role too often assumed, i.e., the clerk who makes sure that all the paper work required by a particular college is completed. Herr and Cramer (1968) discuss the involvement of the counselor in the high school to college transition. What is necessary to note is that the counselor has an important counseling role to play in the implementation phase of the student's vocational or educational choice.

In summary, a comprehensive and longitudinal program offers the greatest potential for successful and meaningful guidance. Beginning at the elementary school level and following through in a coordinated and unified manner to placement of the student in educational or vocational areas at the end of high school has been suggested as a necessity in the school of today. The school through the counselor must provide the necessary personal-social, vocational, and educational information and assistance to students. This may not be the only way that this information and assistance is provided, but it is very appropriate for the school to be involved rather deeply in the process.

Pupil Personnel Services

The type of resource personnel available to the school varies widely. Since ideal situations rarely occur in schools, the counselor often has to adjust his role to fill the greatest need for the greatest number of students. Where student needs are great and resources are scarce, the setting of priorities becomes crucial. The counselor often assumes clerical and administrative roles as well as guidance and counseling roles. There is no question that these kinds of tasks are important. But there is some question as to whether the counselor is the best person to provide them and whether the school is getting the best possible service from its expenditures. In the opinion of the authors, counselor involvement in clerical and administrative tasks is a questionable practice. What is needed is the establishment of priority of tasks related to the training of the counselor and his unique competency. Before dealing with this question it may be of value to explain briefly the potential role of various other specialists in the pupil personnel services program.

School Psychologist

Generally the school psychologist is expected to provide service for those students who require specialized diagnosis or treatment. He also can assist in the referral of special students to more appropriate learning experiences. In some cases the psychologist's activities may overlap with those of a school counselor. This need not be. There is a need to work out the interrelationships between pupil personnel staff. The psychologist has competencies in individual testing, diagnosis of psychological deviation, and child growth and development. With the number of pupils generally assigned to them, most psychologists are not at a loss for clients.

Some general suggestions have been offered for making the input of the psychologist more effective. He can serve as a resource person to teachers. This is especially meaningful at the elementary level as the teacher may be quite effective in assisting pupils to move in more positive directions. The psychologist may also wish to work with groups of students in an attempt to provide an environment where self-understanding and investigation of alternatives and consequences of action can take place.

Social Worker

A second pupil personnel service worker available in many schools is the school social worker. Although the title is different from place to place, the social worker generally provides liaison between the school and other parts of society. School-home relationships often occupy a major portion of the social worker's time. However, there is a need to establish a task area which both fits within the competency of the social worker and the needs of the student population. In the same way that role differentiation is necessary for counselors, psychologists, teachers and school personnel, it is important that the social worker determine a realistic role.

A second area of the social worker's concern is interaction with agency personnel. Whatever program exists within the larger society should be known to the social worker so that relevant referrals can be made and the time between identification of student need and some amelioration of this need is at a minimum. This specifically relates to the concept of a total service orientation which is being suggested by many people presently.

There may be other pupil personnel specialists available to provide specialized service to students. If these people, e.g., attendance personnel, are available, there is a need to work out the task areas in such a way that minimal overlap exists and maximum service is provided.

4

Counselor Preparation for Appalachia

The Present Situation

The plight of the individual in Appalachia is not a new phenomenon; there have been many efforts aimed at providing more meaningful education and guidance for the student in Appalachia. Several studies have suggested that certain characteristics of Appalachian youth are similar to those of urban and suburban youth in areas to which Appalachian familes migrate (Riccio, 1965; Stevic and Uhlig, 1967). The critical variable seems to be the predisposition to move away from Appalachia or perhaps, better stated, the fact that the family has moved to a new location.

However, the previous deprivation often leaves a scar upon the school age youth of the Appalachian family. In addition to the noticeable lack of academic achievement in many cases with its concomitant dislike for things educational, it can be noted that other areas of the person's life are affected. Any service that hopes to have some success in dealing with this problem needs to be comprehensive and longitudinal and to extend beyond natural geographical boundaries. This poses a problem since the Appalachian population is almost always a minority and thus does not have the power to bring about effective change.

Education offers one avenue for the youth to make positive movement toward a more adequate existence. However, education has been conceived in negative terms by the Appalachian resident. He has experienced an educational process which has not met many of his needs. He has experienced teachers who are dedicated but hampered by lack of funds, facilities, and support for education. He has lived his life in a situation where welfare has been a way of life—not a good way, but none the less a way. He has relatives who are still dependent upon someone else to provide support, whether from the "company store" or welfare. He experiences daily an attitude of defeatism, of a gradual depletion of energy to improve his place in life. In short, he sees that all around him are gradually losing the struggle for an independent existence and that some have accepted dependency.

The bright note in this is that the basic characteristic of the people who originally inhabited the Appalachian region was one of independence. In fact, one might suggest that this region was originally settled because it gave a man an opportunity to assert his independence, to meet his own needs in his own ways. One must assume that this characteristic still exists although the manifestation of it may lead to different behaviors or outcomes than it once did.

One attempt at meeting the needs of the Appalachian youth is the Appalachia Educational Laboratory. Founded in the early 1960's, the Laboratory has cooperated with several on-going projects designed to meet the needs of students more effectively. Many of these have to do with transition from school to work although areas such as post-high school education are also a possibility.

An example of the Laboratory's activity is the Counseling and Job Placement Program in Wood County, West Virginia, which began in the summer of 1964 with a two-year grant from the Carnegie Corporation. The program received continuing support from the Appalachia Educational Laboratory during the summer of 1966 for the expressed purpose of disseminating information about its successful operation to other school systems in the region and exploring an approach to the dropout problem. This project listed several objectives which were highly related to guidance programming and which required the involvement of trained counselors, such as: (1) counseling parents and students concerning future vocational and educational needs; (2) establishing a placement center to assist students to obtain part and full-time employment; (3) providing a more realistic link between the students' social and vocational high school activities and their future; (4) involving community employers and industry in this service; (5) encouraging the return to school of those students who left prior to graduation.

As the reader will note, the efforts needed to meet the above objectives are very closely tied to activities in which school counselors have traditionally been engaged. The degree of the problem is probably greater on the average, but the tasks which the counselor is called upon to provide are quite similar.

In addition to the above areas, several others were identified. Teacher involvement was emphasized. The utilization of new methods, materials, and hardware necessitated the involvement of teachers in in-service training and, most importantly, in implementation of the program. Curricular changes were necessary to meet the needs of students. Changes in attitudes by parents and teachers were necessary, and thus self-understanding was an integral part of the programs. Tests were used to aid in self-understanding, groups were organized to deal with changes of behavior and attitude, and summer institutes for teachers to learn new methods and technology were initiated.

Thus, many activities were begun to provide a more meaningful preparation for life for the Appalachian youth. The end is not yet in sight, but at least the problem has been spotlighted. People have been involved and will continue to be involved. In some cases the armamentaria available to the education process have been too little and too late.

Of course there are the normal guidance and counseling programs in many of the schools. These programs generally have the same successes and failures of guidance and counseling programs in other schools. Some students respond well to the educative offerings and are helped to make the decisions and transitions which society seems to demand. Others are relatively unaffected by the offerings within the school and either leave early or bide their time until their formal contact with school is over. Some students respond negatively to the educational experience and are perhaps less well-off after encountering the school than they would be without the experience. Percentages vary in Appalachia as compared to suburban or even urban schools but the student types are somewhat similar. And, as is true in most schools, the counselor cannot serve all the students assigned to him and must establish priorities. Overloading, inadequate understanding of the student, lack of facilities, and lack of funding contribute greatly to the educationally deprived state of too many Appalachian students.

Since it is probably unwise to think that there will be a sufficient increase in the numbers of counselors available to schools in general, the direction which seems most appropriate is to utilize the personnel presently available more advantageously. This suggests that teachers, counselors, other pupil personnel specialists, community personnel, social agency personnel, and para-professionals will be more intimately involved with guidance and counseling aspects as applied to Appalachian youth. The methods used may also need modification so that efficiency as well as achievement are part of the guidance process.

Problems of Maturation of the Student

In many ways the student in Appalachia is more mature than his peer in other areas. He is taught to be independent and self-sustaining relatively early in life. He is pushed to leave the "protected" environment of the home or the school as quickly as possible. However, in some important ways he is also less mature than his counterparts. He is probably not as knowledgeable about himself, his goals, and the total society as his urban counterpart. On several maturation scales he would probably lag behind, e.g., vocational maturity. His responses to vocational choice questionnaires suggest that his choices are determined by glamour rather than relationship to reality factors such as aptitude or availability.

Dealing with Maturation

Certain aspects of maturation may be allowed to develop at less than normal rates. It is at the point that certain personal, vocational and educational decisions need to be made that immaturity is a problem. In order to avoid this there must be certain activities available for students which provide meaningful assistance in this process. The school staff in general, and the counseling staff in particular, will need to be flexible and to approach the situation in other than traditional ways.

Recent research on the occupational maturation of disadvantaged youth (Maynard, 1970; Ansell, 1970) suggests that the typical student in this category is two or more years behind the more "normal" individual in maturation. In these cases certain aspects of maturation can be identified, e.g., readiness for decision-making, and can be provided for in a program. The counselor should be a leader in 1) determining the level at which the individual student is functioning and 2) providing programs and activities to aid the student in more adequate movement toward maturation.

When we discuss physical maturation we may not be faced with the same dilemma as above. However, a problem does exist when the student decides to leave school early and is faced with competing for work with those who are physically more able than he. Obviously it would be better if the individual completed school, thus adding at least two years to the possible maturation time. We are not so certain what might be done for the early leaver except to help him understand the nature of his situation and to provide for continuing interactions when possible or to help him learn appropriate ways of coping with his own existence as well as the environment.

Within school, prior to the students leaving, the use of groups might be valuable. Students with similar concerns can share, in a relatively safe environment, their thoughts and feelings in this area. Similarly the use of modeling might be feasible. Live student models or video tape sessions would provide a foundation for discussion and action on the students' part. Finally, the counselor may utilize reinforcement to increase the probability of certain behaviors of the student. In concert with the student, he can establish goals and move toward these in a personal counseling interaction.

Problems of Motivation of the Student

A crucial factor in the lives of many persons in Appalachia is their degree of motivation to succeed. As one reads about or experiences Appalachia he forms the distinct impression that the people are no longer motivated to succeed by individual effort. In fact, for large segments of the population, it would appear that a supported existence is completely acceptable. This lack of motivation toward accomplishment is manifested early in the lives of many Appalachian children. Education has relatively little meaning as they appraise its relationship to their lives. Parenthetically, it may well be true that the educational process, geared as it often is to the middle group, does not really speak to the needs of Appalachian youth.

The school, through the teaching, pupil personnel, and administrative staff, must deal with the motivational problem. This will probably involve considerable psychological investment on the school personnel's part for it is difficult to deal with persons who openly reject one's values. This is what happens when the student and/or his parent suggest that the values of schooling seen by teachers, counselors, and administrators are generally not relevant to their existence. Further, the student is usually not interested in change. The research of Stevic and Uhlig (1967) suggests that perhaps Appalachian youth do not aspire to some jobs available to them not because they are not motivated to work but because the jobs do not represent as great an income as social welfare existence.

Dealing with Motivation

The counselor will be deeply involved in attempting to motivate the student and to aid him in moving more normally through tasks and developmental levels which lead to maturity. It is apparent that these problems must be faced early in the life of the child. The elementary teacher and administrator may need to adopt the point of view that academic achievement or advancement is not the only criterion for success. Personal growth and, when appropriate, personal introspection are necessary. Students must be aided to see the relevance of education and work as early as possible. In addition, the school must be altered when appropriate to better meet the needs of these students.

Secondly, parental involvement is essential and this must be real involvement, not tokenism. The parent is usually apprehensive when the school seeks his assistance. Too often in the past, Appalachians, as well as other parents, have been used in various service capacities, but their ideas or other positive contributions have not been considered. The school has not been seen in a positive light and this must be offset if we are to move toward meaningful parent involvement. The counselor can be a key person in this process both as an actual contact person and as a resource person to teachers. The counselor can involve the parent in the school life of his child in regard to educational decision-making, i.e., choice of subject, tracks, and so on. He also can aid the teacher to be more skilled in conducting parent conferences. Parent conferences can thus be utilized to increase the general understanding of the school and, one hopes, personal as well as financial support.

Thirdly, the school must begin to deal with those factors which inhibit the child's growth and thus contribute to lack of motivation. The counselor can provide assistance in curricular reform in several ways. He could become the leader in the process although this would detract from many of his counseling tasks. He should be available to curriculum committees to provide information concerning the needs of students as these have become known to him through interviews, follow-up efforts, returning graduates, and new information from other research related to the needs of students and the present social situation. The counselor thus serves as a consultant to those charged with curriculum review and is prepared to provide specific information and ideas for the process.

Finally, the counselor may need to develop a *modus operandi* to deal with lack of motivation. Small group meetings and individual sessions need to be held to provide an opportunity for the student to examine his own needs and goals. There is often a temptation to push one point of view in the area of motivation which is generally definable in a broad societal context. There is nothing wrong with the counselor having certain values, opinions, and so on, but he should be careful that while working with a student the emphasis is upon helping the student come to grips with his own situation and to make the best decision possible based upon adequate information and self-understanding.

Preparation of Personnel

Counselor education has not addressed itself to the problems of specialized preparation of people to work in Appalachia. Examination of counselor education programs of colleges and universities located near or within Appalachia reveals fairly traditional approaches to counselor preparation, namely, certain didactic courses, some practice counseling with the emphasis on interaction, and final placement in a school. While this model has certain advantages, it will probably not meet the needs of large groups of students in Appalachia, especially if we are to provide services on a broader base than the usual one-to-one situation. There are several aspects of the preparation sequence which need to be discussed.

Selection of Potential Counselors

With relatively few exceptions, counselor education programs have been reactive in the area of selection. Rather than attempting to identify those persons who seem to have the greatest promise to perform the tasks of counseling, we have most often felt that we could change the person in certain ways after acceptance into a program. Realizing that this was not always the case, some institutions began to utilize selective retention devices which were designed to provide for review of the potential counselor after a given period of time in the program. Although this has been somewhat successful, it is obvious that too many people complete programs ill-prepared to provide meaningful counseling and guidance assistance to students.

Recently some counseling authorities (Carkhuff and Truax, 1967) have suggested that counseling assistance offered by some "counselors" can be debilitating. It is postulated that the debilitating counselor can be identified and should be either kept out of the counselor preparation program or should be dissuaded somewhere along the line. These two researchers suggest that measuring counselor traits such as warmth, genuineness, and empathy can provide information for selection or retention. The point to be made is that there is a need to become more deeply involved in identifying and actively recruiting people who seem to have the greatest potential for filling the role of counselor and thus meeting the needs of Appalachian youth.

Preparation

The preparation program for counselors must include both didactic and practical experiences. Emphasis must be laid on understanding the characteristics of the student and adult population, on the use of this information about various content areas relating to the needs of students, and on the implementation of programmatic aspects of the guidance effort.

Characteristics of the Population

It is important that the counselor-to-be deal with the uniqueness of the Appalachian population. Although educational, developmental, and general psychology courses are essential, they are not enough. The counselor needs to expend some effort in examining the particular culture in which he wishes to work. Some of his knowledge may come from his own personal experience. However, we should not assume that this is sufficient. A formal method for examining the characteristics should be developed.

Self-Understanding

Throughout any counselor preparation sequence it is of value to aid the student in self-examination in order to move toward self-understanding. This could take many forms ranging from psychoanalysis to a surface exploration of one's values, needs, goals, strengths or weaknesses. The most effective way is probably somewhere in the middle and should be conceived as an on-going portion of the program. The counselor may find that lack of self-understanding is the greatest barrier to effective relationships with other people. Effective relationships are a key factor in success of guidance programs.

Content Areas

The counselor needs to have some understanding of concepts such as vocational development, occupational choice, decision-making, testing, measurement, counseling theory, and guidance and counseling techniques, to name a few of the traditional content courses which counselors have found valuable. These can be presented in many ways and the counselor educator should be constantly alert to the efficacy of his approach and potential directions for change.

Practicum

A dilemma exists in the area of practicum. It is hard to accept the idea that a person can do an effective job as counselor without some previous supervised training in which the emphasis is upon implementation of knowledge in the process of helping other people. However, most practicums are short term and terminal in nature and one wonders at times how much actual change or learning took place as a result of the experience. The negative aspect of this position deals with the lack of breadth and depth possible when the entire experience is compressed into one college term. It would be possible to include an extra practicum experience, but unless this had some programmatic structure the same questions might be raised at the end of the second experience that were originally raised.

It seems essential that the practicum experience extend over a period of time. Perhaps the potential counselor ought to begin this experience at his initial entrance into a program and continue it throughout the preparation period. At appropriate points along the way such concepts as test interpretation would be included as an integral part of the practicum experience. In this way it would be possible to insure that the range of activities we expect of school counselors would be part of his experiential preparation.

Working With Others

As is suggested in several places in this monograph, the successful counselor in Appalachia will be called upon to work cooperatively with agencies, other school personnel, and the community to provide the most meaningful program for the student. Too often this aspect is left to chance in the professional preparation of counselors. We assume that because counselors were teachers they can be effective with teachers in consultative types of relationships. We assume that the public relations skills necessary to deal with the community are part of the counselor's make-up. We assume that knowing about agencies is equivalent to effectively using agencies. We cannot afford this luxury in Appalachia since cooperative effort and sharing of skills is essential. The counselor preparation program should have these elements built into both the didactic and experiential portions of the program.

Follow-Up and Evaluation

Too often we have ignored this part of the work of the counselor. He needs to have some notions about what the graduates or early leavers do or do not do. This information will provide a foundation for more effective functioning in future situations. Similarly, it is of value for the school staff to have some data concerning the effectiveness of the program which is available to students. Both of these activities require some competence on the part of the counselor, which in all probability is obtained most efficiently in a counselor preparation sequence.

Change of Behavior

One of the continuing concerns that plague the school is that which relates to changing the behavior of school personnel when the present behavior is no longer appropriate. This aspect should be considered in the counselor selection-retention process. Does the candidate appear to have some flexibility? Does he appear willing to alter certain directions which are no longer fruitful? In short, does he appear to be a person who can continue to grow and to relate to others in a constructive manner?

This does not solve the problem of the people presently employed by the school who do not manifest this flexibility. The counselor-in-training should receive some training in how one might help people change. This is a slow and tedious process, but the counselor may be in the best position in the school to accomplish it. Therefore, the counselor should begin to see himself as an agent of change.

Behavioral Techniques

One way by which we may be able to improve the counselor's efficiency without decreasing his effectiveness is to utilize behavioral techniques in the helping relationships offered students. This process is designed to aid students and counselors to define goals and to use appropriate methods of reinforcement or reward to move toward those goals. A brief account may help clarify this process. When the student encounters the counselor it is essential that the counselor be prepared to help define or modify goals which the student has. In many cases the goals of the student are implicit rather than explicit and are often based upon an inadequate evaluation of the potential which he has. The counselor must begin to help the student to reexamine his own goals so that they are explicit and "realistic," and then, by reinforcement or reward in words, actions, or products, help the student move toward his goals.

An important facet of counselor behavior when working with Appalachian youth will be to extinguish those behaviors or attitudes that inhibit the counselee's movement toward realistic goals. Thus the counselor will need to ignore negative remarks, inaccurate statements, and goals which are below minimal levels for the student. It will also be important for the counselor to be aware of and work within the social environment of the student. His family, the community, the school, as well as leisure activities, are important forces in shaping negative and positive behavior which may supplement the counselor's efforts.

In summary, the preparation sequence which a counselor goes through ought to prepare him to be a helping person to a wide variety of people. He needs skills to work cooperatively with community groups, agencies, and other school personnel. He needs to understand the characteristics of the population with which he works and the community, both narrowly and widely conceived, in which the students do and will function. He needs to understand change and be willing to act as an agent of change to alter those aspects of the school, the community, and the student's environment which inhibit the student.

5

Guidance for Appalachia

Changing Guidance

To improve the guidance services for Appalachian students, existing programs may need to be changed and new programs initiated. There are several considerations that are necessary in attempting to implement or alter guidance and counseling programs. Johnson (1968) lists the following guidelines for the process of change:

1. Evidence That a Need to Change Exists. The first step is to study the program to identify new or unmet needs. Since the guidance program exists to serve students, it is necessary to obtain evidence of where or how it is falling short of meeting its stated objectives, or indeed whether or not the objectives are still valid. If the guidance program is to fulfill its objectives, i.e., meeting the needs of students, it is necessary to obtain evidence or a knowledge of what the needs are.

2. Availability of Personnel and Time. The best designed and planned program modification will not get off the ground unless sufficiently trained staff with time to do the job is available to institute and maintain the change. No guidance program can be optimally successful with inadequately prepared personnel attempting to provide services in unrealistic periods of time. Thus, numbers of persons to be available in addition to the quality of the person and the time limitations must be clearly understood.

3. *Adequacy of Facilities, Equipment, Materials, and Budget to Implement the Change.* In addition to staff and time, most program modifications require facilities, equipment, materials or money, without which the program is likely to founder. The people planning the change must leap this hurdle before they can get new activities under way. Without adequate funding the prospect for effective guidance services is slim.

4. *Establishment of a Climate for Change.* Timing is important for effective program development. The guidance staff, the administration, teachers, students, and parents must be ready for the change. If the people involved are not prepared to accept the change and cooperate in its successful development, the plan is very likely to fail. The school staff and community members must accept the need for guidance services if there is to be a prospect for success. If they do not, the guidance program is likely to be ineffective at best.

Another consideration in the area of initiation, implementation, or alteration of guidance services relates to the broad area of decision-making. Hill (1965) discusses one facet of this consideration when he suggests that most people accept the need for decisions to be made somewhere in an administrative organization and that many people are happy to allow others this privilege. However, while one person is often given the responsibility for the decision, there is a need to utilize as much information and as many people as possible in the steps leading to the decision. The following paraphrased statements are suggested:

> He (decision-maker) must be an idea man.
> The decision-maker must be an idea receiver.
> The decision-maker must be a coordinator of purposes.
> The decision-maker must be a coordinator of roles.
> The decision-maker must seek understanding and support.
> The decision-maker must be a recruiter, selector, and placer of staff.
> The decision-maker must have counseling and mediation skills.

The reader should note that the title "decision-maker" has been substituted for "administrator" in the above statements. Regardless of the wording it finally reaches the crucial point that a decision must be made by someone and the remaining people in the organization must support the direction suggested by the decision.

A second facet of the decision-making process is directed to a special part of the above discussion, i.e., who is the decision-maker in the school organization? Educational administrative theorists suggest that this is a crucial point in understanding an organization and that oftentimes the organizational chart does not provide the necessary information. The guidance worker must have skill in determining this factor. At present there seems to be no way to determine this besides trial and error and intensive observation. As the state of the art improves we may be able to specify with more preciseness where, how, and by whom the critical decisions are made. The counselor should be aware of the necessity of recognizing the decision-maker, especially if he wishes to initiate programs or to alter the status of services within the school.

Guidance for Appalachian Youth

Guidance activities which meet the needs of youth must be founded upon an understanding of the characteristics and needs of the target population. Programmatic aspects are important in the consideration of the provision of guidance services. Thus, one must know who is receiving the services and have some way of altering, individualizing, and increasing the scope of the services in addition to some sequential aspects. Counselors are often called upon to provide a wide range of services for the student. These fall under the following general categories.

Identification

The talents, strengths, weaknesses, aptitudes, abilities, and so forth which each student possesses are of considerable importance in helping him make relevant decisions and choices. Several methods may be used. The school may have an established testing program which provides some of the above information. The counselor should serve as interpreter for persons making use of these tests. Too often the involvement has been as a test giver, scorer, and recorder, and little, if anything, is done in the areas of use of tests and interpretation to the student or others who may have meaning in his life.

It is important to note that tests may not have complete validity for this specific population and thus some compensation in interpretation or change of tests seems called for. The counselor needs to spend some time and effort in determining the most appropriate set of tests for the population of the school he serves. He needs to have some plan of operation to get this altered when necessary.

Self-Understanding

One of the more important areas in counseling is that dealing with self-concept. Many definitions might be suggested for this term, but in general it is used to describe the understanding one has of himself.

Generally we deal with this only when there are major discrepancies between what might be called reality and the self-understanding of the student. We can and should be concerned with sharpening each person's awareness of himself, his relationship to his world presently conceived, and his potential for the future. This becomes crucial when the counselor deals with culturally different youth, since he must somehow move into the frame of reference of his counselee and operate from this point of departure.

Values

The counselor needs to provide assistance to the student in the continual examination of his own personal values. This becomes somewhat difficult in many cases since the counselor's value system may conflict or at least differ from that of the counselee. The counselor need not alter his own values, but he must be careful that he does not impose these upon a client who has a different set of values. Thus, the counselor needs to understand his own values and in addition must deal with the client's value system.

Decision-Making

The typical junior and senior high school student is called upon to make a wide variety of decisions. These may range from very simple decisions, e.g., what clothes to wear to school, to very complex decisions, e.g., what the implications of education are to future vocational goals. Admittedly, people have been making these types of decisions for a long time without focusing upon the process to the degree suggested here. However, in our complex society individuals need decision-making skills. There are various ways that decision-making can be facilitated and some of these will be discussed later. The counselor needs to understand the decision-making process so that he can provide assistance to the student as he faces the variety of decisions he will be called upon to make.

Information Services

The counselor, in light of the above discussion, needs to provide up-to-date materials and services to assist the student in making his decisions. Various commercial and non-commercial products are available. In addition, the counselor needs to know the local situation both in terms of what is available and what the graduate or non-graduates of the school do upon separation from school. This means knowledge of the local situation and perhaps contacts within the local community to get immediate information when necessary. Lest the reader assume that we are prescribing a complete service without the student's involvement, let us hasten to point out that we are not. What is suggested is that the counselor point out sources of information and then help the student make sense of it in light of his (the student's) present and future world.

Motivation

One of the most critical facets of the lives of people in Appalachia and other similar situations is a lack of motivation. Regardless of the causes of their low level of motivation, it is essential that the school begin to deal with this problem. Traditional urgings and exhortations will probably not do the job. We shall try to suggest some ways in a later section of this monograph.

Guidance Services

Meaningful guidance and counseling programs for Appalachian schools are not greatly different from guidance and counseling programs in other schools. Some of the problems or concerns which students face in Appalachia are unique, however, and individualized programmatic arrangements must be made. The specific requirements are listed below.

Longitudinal Integrated Service

In order to be effective, guidance service ought to be provided on a continuing basis. If we wait for the student to get to high school before we begin to provide assistance to him in understanding his own personal characteristics and to begin to deal with such factors as decision-making, developmental growth, and interpersonal dynamics, we have lost valuable time. In Appalachia we may have lost many of the students who have already left school.

There is a need to provide assistance as early as possible in the student's life. This means that elementary school guidance is essential. In addition, the succeeding levels must be aware of and integrated with the services provided at the preceding level. This means that there needs to be an overlapping program which fosters intercommunication and cooperation among and between pupil personnel specialists. Obviously the people assigned to these positions need to be able to function cooperatively.

Community Involvement

The concept of a total package of service is essential for successful individual assistance to Appalachian youth. The efforts of cooperative community endeavors in school-related activities have been demonstrated to have value. In addition to being able to provide more facilities and services, these efforts have pinpointed the availability of already existing agencies and how these can be of value. The counseling personnel, along with the rest of the school staff, must be aware of these opportunities and must be willing and able to utilize them effectively. Again, this ought to be part of the selection criteria and needs to be included in training programs.

Student Characteristics Data

Much of what we assume about Appalachian youth needs verification. The counselor, regardless of the school level at which he functions, is in an advantageous position to provide leadership in this area. We need to know more about the developmental patterns and levels of Appalachian youth. We need to know more about attitudes, how these are formed, what differentiates graduates from non-graduates. We need to discover the pattern of employment, education, or training following school-leaving, whether caused by graduation or not. In short, we need to be more aware of what the student is like, what happens to him in and out of school, and in what direction he goes after leaving school.

In the same general framework we need to know what is available to the student upon leaving school. What jobs or educational opportunities are obtainable within the immediate environment? What opportunities exist elsewhere? How can these be linked most effectively? The counselor again can take a leadership position in attempting to acquire and organize this data. No suggestion is made that this become mechanical. The student must be aided to plan his future, to understand alternatives, and to move in meaningful directions.

Testing and the Appalachian Student

A meaningful testing program in Appalachian schools must include early and comprehensive measurement of potential, ability level, and achievement. In addition, individual students may require specialized testing in the form of interest check lists and, in some cases, personality assessment. The latter two require special attention, and the counselor should be aware of the limitations in the use of these types of tests. Wholesale use of either interest check lists or personality tests is not advocated.

Achievement and Ability Testing

There is a close relationship between these two types of tests. Ability tests are usually designed to measure potential for academic success.

In many cases certain cultural aspects affect the score which a student attains. In all probability the actual score which an Appalachian student receives is below his real ability level. However, this need not affect the use of the test for counseling purposes, since we still have data which are helpful to us in planning programs and providing assistance to youth. When we determine that a student is above or below average in ability regardless of the norms we use we can plan more realistic programs for him.

At the same time that we administer ability tests we should also gather information concerning achievement levels. These data can be of considerable individual value. We often find that students score below national, local, or grade norms on achievement tests. If this signals underachievement we are called upon to provide specialized individual academic assistance. However, if we find that the student is functioning at about the level his ability predicts, even though below some norm, other alternatives in addition to academic bolstering may be signaled. Thus, we need to know both ability and achievement levels in order to make the most efficient use of tests.

In terms of administration of tests it is important that time of year and school level be considered. It seems that the most appropriate time for achievement and ability testing is early in the academic year. This is suggested for two reasons. First, it avoids the negative perception by many teachers that the test is an evaluation of his performance for the year. It thereby avoids teaching to a test. Secondly, the test data are more up-to-date in the fall and can be used as diagnostic tools by teachers. The counselor should take the lead in this method of using achievement and ability testing. The teacher can become more effective in helping students, first by strengthening areas in which students are below expectations and, secondly, by dealing with variations of achievement manifested by students. It is recommended that achievement tests be given every year and that ability tests be given every three years.

There is a need to evaluate the testing program on a regular basis. The objectives of the teacher or a specific content area may change. These changes should be taken into account in any testing program. The counselor should provide leadership in the organization and use of the testing program.

A further consideration is necessary as the student moves into secondary school. Especially during his junior and senior years he may be subjected to numerous external tests, e.g., PSAT. There is an issue here concerning over-testing and the counselor should be involved in the determination of the priority of need for test data. Many schools may opt to discontinue the internal ability and achievement testing during the last two years of secondary school.

Aptitude Testing

The Appalachian student needs to have information about his aptitudes, i.e., the potential he has in certain skill areas. It is best to wait until late junior or early senior high school to administer this type of test. One reason for waiting is that the student may have little interest in the area and thus may not make a serious effort on the exam. There is also some question concerning maturity, personal development, and aptitude scores. The test and results should have some meaning for the student, or there is some question concerning its inclusion in a testing sequence.

As with the ability and achievement tests, the results of aptitude tests are most valuable when used to aid the student to more meaningful planning and self-understanding. It is important that the student know why the test is being given, what is being measured, and how he does on the particular test. Too often none of these three factors is included in the testing program.

It would be of value to the student to relate the results of the aptitude test to the possibilities within the local geographic area. However, in many cases the counselor, or someone familiar with the job market, will have to deal with a broader concept of work, including possibilities in other geographic areas.

Interest and Personality Assessment

Although the counselor should have competence in the use and interpretation of interest and personality assessment instruments, some caution should be exercised in their use. These types of "tests" should be administered when the information provided by these tests will be valuable to continuing growth by the student. Some interest and personality instruments have relatively little potential and possibly harmful content, and many deeply interested people see a problem in the wholesale assessment of interest and personality. The counselor should know the instruments, be familiar with what is being measured, and be able to provide effective interpretive assistance to the student. He needs to know the limitations of all tests, especially interest and personality instruments.

Specific Tests

We have avoided naming specific tests which might be recommended in the various areas. It is important that the counseling and teaching staff develop a testing program based upon the specific needs of the school and the student body. Test publishers will provide technical assistance to any school or school district which may be planning to institute a new testing program. This process, it seems to us, will be more productive and effective than a testing program which is the product of an outside person without in-depth knowledge of the local situation.

Summary

Testing is an important aspect of a functional guidance program in Appalachia. The student needs to understand his strengths and weaknesses, to investigate possible alternatives, and to make educational and vocational decisions. A properly organized and administered testing program, including achievement, ability, and aptitude tests and, in certain instances, personality and interest instruments, is essential. Parents, teachers, counselors, students, and administrators should be involved in the selection of tests, and there must be general acceptance of the value and use of the testing program. Finally, if the student does not understand why the tests were given and how he did on them, there is a serious question as to whether or not the testing program should be continued.

Counseling with Appalachian Students

A brief description of a behavioral approach to counseling may be in order, since it seems to be suitable for the Appalachian student.

Krumboltz (1966) asserts that "the goals of counseling must be stated in terms of specific behavior changes desired by each individual client and agreed to by his counselor." Once the goal or goals have been established, methods of accomplishing them are defined. In general, there are four approaches which can be identified.

The first of these is operant learning. In this case behavior is learned or modified by providing reinforcement as quickly as possible after the proper behavior has occurred. The behavior, once learned, continues as long as some periodic reinforcement is given. Thus, students learn to write certain types of papers for certain teachers because their proper behavior was once reinforced. It seems quite probable that the counselor may be a reinforcing agent.

The second possible process is that of imitative learning. The most obvious method here is to provide models for the counselee to observe and to imitate. The counselor again can reinforce certain bits and pieces of that behavior which is most appropriate according to the goals which have been established. Live models or the use of edited videotaped models are the usual methods for modeling behavior.

The third area is that of cognitive learning. In general, this refers to the advice giving or information presentation by the counselor to a counselee who seems ready and willing to accept this. The fact of the matter is that many clients probably see this as a most appropriate counselor behavior. In the cognitive learning area we would include the concept of contracts. Although this can take many forms it generally means that a "contract" to do certain things is accepted by the counselee in return for assistance by the counselor or teacher. The student is expected to "play" a certain "role" with the general outcome being a learned behavior more adequate to the needs of the student in his own personal, social, or family environment.

The final method is emotional learning. This approach is the more classical conditioning application in which client reactions are altered by pairing the stimuli which elicits the anxiety or emotional reaction with a more pleasant stimuli. The counselor may help the client relax and then present anxiety-producing stimuli in a gradually increasing fashion in order to help the client to be able to overcome the anxiety. Other possibilities exist in this area but these are generally useable with more extreme cases of maladaptive behavior and the school counselor may have less opportunity to apply this technique.

It is probable that parts of all four processes will be used at various times. The important factors seem to be that goals are established cooperatively between client and counselor and that the necessary reinforcers are identified so that when appropriate behavior occurs, reinforcement can follow quickly.

The process described herein is presented in rather simplistic terms. The Appalachian counselor can learn to utilize this process effectively if he is willing to devote some time to learning the principles and practicing the technique. We believe that the time spent in such activities will be well spent since behavioral counseling seems to be more efficient and effective than other approaches.

There is one further item which needs to be discussed in the category of counseling Appalachian youth. This relates to the migration which has been taking place and which will probably increase. As we suggested earlier, the Appalachian migrant generally goes to a large urban area. Once there, he often finds himself as isolated as he was back in Appalachia. The isolation is psychological and personal rather than geographical. He is among other Appalachians, but he has little access to the avenues of assistance in the city. He finds himself with new concerns or problems to resolve but with little knowledge as to where he might seek answers or resolution. There are two actions which will help eliminate this problem. First, the school should provide assistance to the student while he is enrolled in school. He needs to understand what faces him as he moves out of Appalachia. He needs to know what is available in terms of services normally offered in urban areas. He needs to know how to relate to these services. This information can be made available by the counselor and, in addition, should be explained whenever appropriate.

It is also necessary for the social agencies in urban areas to be attuned to the special needs of the Appalachian migrant. The social agency contact person needs to understand the background of the migrant. He needs to be able to relate to him in meaningful ways and to offer assistance on relatively short notice. He, above all, needs to be aware that the migrant is in the urban area. Thus, the social agency worker needs to be sensitive to the nature of the Appalachian migrant and be willing to provide assistance to him.

Educational and Vocational Planning with Appalachian Students

We have suggested earlier that education is not afforded value and respect by Appalachian youth. In many cases the student has only tolerated education and has escaped from it as early as possible. Parents have not supported educational excellence for their schools nor promoted it in their homes. Therefore, education has not been seen as a vital force in the lives of most Appalachian youth. This is changing somewhat with the establishment of regional laboratories where more meaningful educational experiences are provided, but non-support of the value of education is still the most dominant theme.

Educational planning at all levels must receive greater attention. The counselor is in an advantageous position to provide this assistance. Beginning with the student's first opportunity to make curriculum decisions, the counselor should stress the process of educational planning. In many schools the counselor's involvement is limited to superficial and mechanical aspects of scheduling. In these cases he is missing an opportunity to provide valuable assistance to the student in relating his interests, abilities, and aptitudes to the choices available within the school. Parents can be involved in this process if the school is willing to make allowance for this. Obviously, any educational decision is one step in a total vocational decision.

The student also needs to be aware of post high school possibilities. College is one of these, but not the only choice. Technical schools, community colleges, junior colleges, trade schools, and many other possibilities exist in almost every area. The counselor needs to have a thorough knowledge of what is available and must be able to communicate this information to students.

The same set of circumstances exists for vocational choices. The counselor must know the local situation and be able to help students deal effectively with the opportunities or lack of them. The student will have to deal with the broader situation in his vocational planning. He may reach the position that he may have to leave his home region in order to find job possibilities which most closely relate to his needs. He must understand various aspects of vocational development, e.g., entry level positions, the structure of occupations, and career development. He will need assistance in applying these to his own situation.

The counselor must have available information about the job market within and outside the area. He will probably need to purchase some of the materials available from publishing companies which provide information about colleges and jobs. He will need to see his job as including personal assistance in the area of decision-making and should follow up students who leave the high school and go on to higher education or vocational activities.

Within the framework of behavioral counseling this type of assistance can be offered. The counselor can utilize reinforcement of information to promote the student's movement toward educational or vocational goals. He may wish to utilize models, adults, and other students to provide information to the student as he attempts to order his life.

Summary

We are proposing that the needs of the Appalachian youth are similar to the needs of the majority of culturally different youth and that these are not significantly different from all youth. In those areas where unique needs or differences occur, the guidance program must be altered to provide the most meaningful service possible. Thus, when students have little or no motivation toward educational or occupational tasks, the school program in general, and guidance in particular, should promote those activities which increase motivation or perhaps which inhibit the factors causing lack of motivation.

The community and state are meaningful entities when the needs of Appalachia are considered. First, there is a need for cooperative efforts among various agencies and components to provide the facilities and comprehensive program which are indicated. Secondly, the financial support necessary for the program must be generated, to a great extent from outside. Without input of money the chances of creating an educational program to meet the needs of the people of Appalachia are very poor.

The Coordinated Approach to Guidance in Appalachia

Jaques (1970) suggests that the programs designed to unite rehabilitation and education require the use of developmental concepts on three coordinated levels of planning of service: (1) Prevention, (2) Intervention, and (3) Follow-up and Evaluation. One could easily expand this to the broader base that all community agencies, rehabilitation, social, and employment services, and schools, need to cooperate to provide the most meaningful and relevant assistance to youth. This is especially true for the youth from Appalachia since it is impossible to delineate problems and solve them without cooperative efforts from several different helping persons.

This, of course, suggests that new methods of communication need to be developed between the various agencies. The school counselor, regardless of level of operation, is in a most advantageous position to institute and promote this cooperation. The entire concept presupposes that there is an understanding of the various services available. Obviously, facilities, funds, and personnel are also important prerequisites. In many cases there will be inadequacies in one, several, or all of the areas, and priority-setting will be important. The focus of the helping profession is on the individual as he attempts to move toward optimum functioning. Whatever is needed in the adjustment of the individual to his environment and the adjustment of the environment to the individual should be readily available. In many cases the problem is not lack of available service but rather, lack of knowledge concerning the availability of the service.

The school counselor should take a brief period of time to acquaint himself with the types of agencies and service personnel available within and outside the school. He should not be hesitant to contact the various agencies since it is obvious that he and his fellow counselors cannot provide all the assistance which students in the schools may require. It has been pointed out by Wright (1959) that about 10% of the population of the school might be eligible for rehabilitation services, including, in some cases, financial support. This same suggestion is probably true when one considers social agencies, health agencies, employment agencies, and so on. Thus, the counselor can promote a broadened approach to assist students by the simple act of identifying what is available and being willing to contact some of these agencies when student needs appear to exist. There is no suggestion in the above that the counselor should abdicate his particular responsibilities by referring students to someone else. Nor is there an intention to suggest that the counselor do all the necessary work to insure the successful completion of a referral. He must be able to assist when it is appropriate. State departments of education often offer assistance in this area, at least in terms of information about agencies and opportunities.

A ramification of the coordinated approach concerning youth from Appalachia is that the need may extend beyond the immediate community. Many people leave Appalachia seeking better opportunities elsewhere. Although many do succeed in this goal, others find that the despair and poverty they knew in Appalachia have been transplanted to an urban setting. They most certainly are no better off and perhaps, since they must cope with a very hostile environment, the situation is worse. It is incumbent upon school personnel and other agency personnel to deal with this added factor in the life of the transplanted Appalachian. They should help prepare those people leaving Appalachia to understand the new situation and aid them in beginning to develop ways of coping with the people, as well as the social, economic, and environmental situation they will face.

Outside Agencies

The above suggests that the counselor cannot expect to accomplish the job himself. Many other people will need to cooperate if the student is to be helped in setting and moving toward realistic goals. The concept of regional laboratories with specialists and consultants obviously is directed to this need. There are other aspects of outside agency assistance which need to be discussed.

An outside agency is defined within the context of this monograph as any potential aid offered outside the school program. This could include parent organizations; local, regional, or state rehabilitation agencies; vocational centers; in short, those formal or informal groups which could offer specialized assistance to the student. The counselor needs to know about these opportunities. It would be fruitless, if not impossible, to describe every possibility. A description of some major types might help.

Rehabilitation Agencies

Various rehabilitation agencies, under the auspices of the Federal or state government, exist in most areas. Basically, these are designed to provide rehabilitation for individuals who have disabilities. Fortunately, this concept has been expanded to include physical, psychological, mental, and other types of disabilities, so that these are generally available to provide service to larger numbers of people. Each agency is staffed by a trained professional with knowledge of psychological development, motivation, and learning and the ability to help clients more effectively deal with their concerns in areas of disability. The variety of services available through rehabilitation agencies is great, and the counselor needs to develop an understanding of the rehabilitation agency, preferably during his preparation period.

Mental Health Agencies

These community agencies are designed to provide assistance to persons with personality disorders. In many cases the staff of these agencies includes case workers, psychologists, and counselors who have training and competency in the helping relationship, and they can be a valuable adjunct to the school in providing service to the individual student as well as his family. It is generally true that these types of agencies have access to more highly skilled personnel, such as psychiatrists, for consultation and treatment assistance.

Social Agencies

Most counties or communities have several different types of social agencies designed to provide specific services to the residents of the particular area. Some examples are Aid to Dependent Children, the Legal Aid Association, and the Children's Aid Society. Each county or geographic area will differ in the types and numbers of such agencies. In most cases the information concerning what is available to the population of the community is included in a regularly revised directory. The school ought to have this information available and, in addition, have someone who is familiar with the various agencies so that when assistance is called for, "immediate" referral can be made.

Service Clubs

Many of the service clubs, e.g., Lions, have taken special interest in the physical and psychological needs of people. These organizations provide these specific services at little or no cost to people in need of them. Most have representatives assigned to cover the school, and so the counselor need only contact this representative to take advantage of what is offered. The counselor may need to develop a list of these organizations and then identify the contact person. This is relatively easy but could be extremely beneficial to the students in the particular school.

Federal and State Agencies

The Federal and state governments have established many agencies which could assist the school. State Departments of Health, State Departments of Public Welfare, State Departments of Education, State

Schools for Special Children, and the U.S. Department of Health, Education and Welfare, are examples. The staffs of these agencies are charged with various responsibilities which relate closely to the educational needs of students. In many cases there is financial as well as consultative assistance available to schools and school personnel from these agencies.

In short, the availability of outside resources is extremely great. The student often does not receive his full share of service either because the particular agency is not known to him or because community resources have been overlooked. A team approach to service must be brought to bear on the problems which students have so that these problems can be resolved.

BIBLIOGRAPHY

Ansell, Edgar M., An Assessment of Vocational Maturity of Lower-class Caucasians, Lower-class Negroes and Middle-class Caucasians in Grades Eight Through Twelve. Doctoral dissertation, State University of New York at Buffalo, 1970.

Ball, Richard, "A Poverty Case: the Analgesic Subculture of the Southern Appalachians." *American Sociological Review*, 1968, 33, pp. 884–894.

Brewer, Earl, "Religion and the Churches," in *The Southern Appalachian Region*, T. Ford (Ed.). Lexington: University of Kentucky Press, 1962.

Caudill, Harry, "Misdeal in Appalachia." *The Atlantic Monthly*, June 1965, 215, pp. 43–47.

———, *Night Comes to the Cumberlands*. Boston: Little, Brown and Company, 1963.

Ernst, Harry, "Appalachians in a Hostile World." *Sunday-Gazette Mail*, Charleston, West Virginia, October 9, 1966.

Ford, T., "Status, Residence, and Fundamentalist Religious Beliefs in Southern Appalachia." *Social Forces*, October 1960, pp. 41–49.

———, *The Southern Appalachian Region*. Lexington: University of Kentucky Press, 1962.

Goldman, Leo, "Group Guidance: Content and Process." *Personnel and Guidance Journal*, 1962, 40 (6), pp. 518–522.

Herr, Edwin L., and Cramer, Stanley H., *Guidance of the College-bound: Problems, Practices and Perspectives*. New York: Appleton-Century-Crofts, 1968.

Hill, George E., *Management and Improvement of Guidance*. New York: Appleton-Century-Crofts, 1965.

Hooker, Elizabeth, *Religion in the Highlands: Native Churches and Missionary Enterprises in the Southern Appalachian Area*. New York: Home Missions Council, 1933.

Jaques, Marceline E., "Rehabilitation Counseling: Scope and Services," *Guidance Monograph Series*. Boston: Houghton Mifflin Company, 1970.

John, Bruce, "Appalachia—Problems and Solutions," *Extension Reader Series*, no. 93. Morgantown: Cooperative Extension Services, West Virginia University, 1965.

Johnson, Dorothy E., "Expanding and Modifying Guidance Programs," *Guidance Monograph Series.* Boston: Houghton Mifflin Company, 1968.

Kaplan, Berton, "The Structure of Adaptive Sentiments in a Lower-class Religious Group in Appalachia." *The Journal of Social Issues,* January 1965, pp. 126–141.

Krumboltz, John D. (Ed.), *Revolution in Counseling.* Boston: Houghton Mifflin Company, 1966.

Looff, David, *Psychiatric Perspective on Poverty in America.* Lexington: University of Kentucky Medical Center, 1968.

Loughary, J. W., Stripling, R. O., and Fitzgerald, P. W. (Eds.), *Counseling: A Growing Profession.* Washington, D.C.: American Personnel and Guidance Association, 1967, pp. 100–106.

Mangalam, Joseph, *Poverty and Occupational Adjustment in Eastern Kentucky.* Lexington: University of Kentucky, 1965.

Mayer, Frank, "Teachers from Appalachia." *School and Society,* October 1966, *19*, pp. 324–325.

Maynard, Peter, Assessing the Vocational Maturity of Inner-city Youths. Unpublished doctoral dissertation, State University of New York at Buffalo, 1970.

Miernyk, William, "Appalachia's Future: the Economic Challenge," *Extension Reader Series,* no. 177. Morgantown: Cooperative Extension Service, West Virginia University, 1968.

Nesius, Ernest, "The Role of the Church in Appalachia," *Extension Reader Series,* no. 128. Morgantown: Cooperative Extension Service, West Virginia University, 1966.

Ogletree, James, "Appalachian Schools—a Case of Consistency," *Extension Reader Series,* no. 179. Morgantown: Cooperative Extension Service, West Virginia University, 1968.

Poinsett, Alex, "Poverty amid Plenty." *Ebony,* August 1965, pp. 105–112.

Riccio, Anthony C., "Occupational Aspirations of Migrant Adolescents from the Appalachian South." *Vocational Guidance Quarterly,* 1965, *14,* pp. 26–30.

Schrag, Peter, "Appalachia: Again a Forgotten Land." *Saturday Review,* January 27, 1968, pp. 14–18.

Schwarzweller, Harry, *Adaptation of Appalachian Migrants to the Industrial Work Situation: A Case Study.* Morgantown: Appalachian Center, West Virginia University, 1969.

Schweiker, William, *Some Facts and a Theory of Migration.* Morgantown: Appalachian Center, West Virginia University, 1968.

Stevic, Richard, and Uhlig, George, "Occupational Aspirations of Selected Appalachian Youth." *Personnel and Guidance Journal,* 1967, *45* (5), pp. 435–439.

Stewart, Lawrence H., and Warnath, Charles F., *The Counselor and Society: A Cultural Approach.* Boston: Houghton Mifflin Company, 1965.

Stuart, Jesse, *The Thread That Runs So True.* New York: Scribners, 1949.

Sweeney, John, "Transportation in Appalachian Development," *Extension Reader Series,* no. 178. Morgantown: Cooperative Extension Service, West Virginia University, 1968.

The Wood County Summer Counseling and Job Placement Program, Appalachia Educational Laboratory, Inc., 1967.

Truax, C. B., and Carkhuff, R. R., *Toward Effective Counseling and Psychotherapy Training and Practice.* Chicago: Aldine Publishing Company, 1967.

Truax, William E., "Critical Requirements of Small School Counselors." *Personnel and Guidance Journal,* 1956, 35 (2), pp. 103–106.

Weller, Jack E., "A Profile of the Appalachian Family," *Extension Reader Series,* no. 180. Morgantown, West Virginia: Cooperative Extension Service, West Virginia University, 1968.

———, "Is There a Future for Yesterday's People?" *Saturday Review,* October 16, 1965a, pp. 33–36.

———, *Yesterday's People.* Lexington: University of Kentucky Press, 1965b.

Wright, George N., "Wanted: More Referrals from High School." *Journal of Rehabilitation,* 1959, 25, pp. 22–23.

Zeller, Fredrick, *Opportunity and Action in Appalachia.* Morgantown: Appalachian Center, West Virginia University, 1967.

INDEX

Ability tests, 59–61
Achievement tests, 59–61
Adjustment to work, 27, 28
Aggressive behavior, 9
Anger, 17
Ansell, E., 47, 71
Appalachia:
    characteristics of, 51
    Regional Development Act, 3
    student characteristics, 44
    teacher, 28
    value system, 7–8
Aptitude test, 61
ASCA, 32
Aspiration of Appalachian students, 25
Ball, R., 8, 9, 71
Behavioral approach to counseling, 52–53, 62–63
Brewer, E., 14, 71
Carkhuff, R., 50, 72
Caudill, H., 1, 6, 14, 19, 71
Change:
    in guidance, 23
    in school, 22
Coal industry, 3
Cognitive learning, 63
Community effort, 58–59
Community involvement in schools, 31
Consultation, 52
Cooperative services, 66
Counselor:
    self-understanding, 51
    values, 49
Cramer, S., 41, 71
Curriculum, 31
Curriculum development, 49
Decision making, 40, 49, 55, 57
Dependency relationships, 3
Economic revival in Appalachia, 4–5
Education, 4
Educational planning, 64
Elementary and Secondary Education Act, 22–23

Elementary school guidance, 37–39
    consultation, 38
    coordination, 38–39
    counseling, 37–38
Emotional learning, 63
Employment, 25
Ernst, H., 26, 71
Evaluation, 52
Family structure of Appalachia, 10–11
Federal agencies, 68–69
Federal funds, 23, 45
Fitzgerald, P., 72
Fixation, 8
Folk culture, 5–6
Ford, T. 5, 16, 71
Frustration, 8, 10
Goldman, L., 31, 71
Group processes, 31
Guidance information, 57
Guidance materials, 57
Helping person, 53
Herr, E., 41, 71
Hill, G., 55, 71
Hooker, E., 71
Infants, 12
Initiative learning, 62
Innovation, 23
Interest inventories, 61
Isolation, 6
Jaques, M., 66, 71
John, B., 2, 6, 71
Johnson, D., 54, 72
Junior high guidance, 39
Kaplan, B., 16, 17, 72
Krumboltz, J., 62, 72
Longitudinal guidance services, 58
Looff, D., 12, 72
Loughary, J., 72
Mangalam, J., 25, 72
Marriage, 13
Maturation, 47–48
Mayer, F., 29, 72
Maynard, P., 47, 72

Mental health agencies, 68
Middle school guidance, 39
Miernyk, W., 5, 72
Migrants, 25
Migration problems, 63–64
Mobility, 29
Motivation, 48, 58
Nepotism, 21–22
Nesius, E., 14, 72
Ogletree, J., 20, 23, 72
Operant learning, 62
Parent consultation, 33
Parent involvement, 49
Peer group influence, 39
Personality inventories, 61
Physical maturation, 47–48
Poinsett, A., 72
Political situation, 18–19
Practice counseling, 51–52
Preventive guidance, 35–36
Programmatic guidance, 32
Promotional guidance, 35, 37
Public relations, 34
Pupil personnel services, 41
Regressive behavior, 9
Rehabilitation, 66–68
Religion, 14–15
Remedial guidance, 35–36
Repression, 13
Research, 34
Resignation, 9
Revival, 15
Riccio, A., 28, 44, 72
School psychologist, 42
School social worker, 42–43

School system, 20
Schrag, P., 2, 72
Schwarzweller, H., 28, 72
Schweiker, W., 25, 72
Secondary school guidance, 41
Selection of counselors, 50
Self concept, 56–57
Service organization, 68
Social agencies, 26, 33, 67–68
State agencies, 68–69
Stevic, R., 25, 44, 48, 72
Stewart, L., 35, 72
Stripling, R., 72
Stuart, J., 22, 73
Student characteristics:
 identification, 56
 intermediate school level, 39
 maturation, 47
Student guidance services, 30
Sweeney, J., 3, 73
Teacher involvement in guidance, 46
Testing, 59
Truax, C., 50, 73
Truax, W., 30, 73
Uhlig, G., 25, 44, 48, 72
Values, 57
Value system, 25
Vocational choice, 65
Vocational development, 47
Warnath, C., 35, 72
Weller, J., 5, 11, 13, 20, 24, 73
Work, attitude toward, 26
Wright, G., 66, 73
Zeller, F., 29, 73